Bloomsbury Professional Tax Insight

Family Investment Companies

Bloomsbury Professional Tax Insight

Family Investment Companies

Second Edition

Deborah Clark

Partner Mills & Reeve LLP

Bloomsbury Professional

LONDON • DUBLIN • EDINBURGH • NEW YORK • NEW DELHI • SYDNEY

BLOOMSBURY PROFESSIONAL

Bloomsbury Publishing Plc

50 Bedford Square, London, WC1B 3DP, UK

1385 Broadway, New York, 10018, USA

Bloomsbury Publishing Ireland Ltd

29 Earlsfort Terrace, Dublin 2, D02 AY28, Ireland

Printed 2024, Reprinted 2024, Reprinted 2025 (twice), Reprinted 2026

5

British Library Cataloguing-in-Publication Data

A catalogue record for this book is available from the British Library.

ISBN: PB: 978 1 52652 469 0

Typeset by Compuscript Ltd, Shannon
Printed and bound by TJ Books, Padstow

MIX
Paper | Supporting responsible forestry
FSC® C013056

Preface

Welcome to the second edition of this book which is an introduction to the subject of family investment companies ('FICs'). It is intended to provide an overview of all the key issues to consider when exploring if a FIC is a suitable vehicle to help with an individual's estate planning. I am delighted that this edition includes some new chapters, the first is by Steve Collings and covers accounting issues and the second by Adam Cooper deals with valuation issues. There is also a new chapter that considers in more detail the estate planning benefits of a FIC. The book also covers issues on how to fund the structure, what tax issues to watch out for, what rights you might give to the shares and the pros and cons of different choices. It is intended to be a practical guide, dealing with directors' powers, the use of an unlimited company and issues around privacy and wealth protection. It concludes with some examples of different structures and explores their benefits and disadvantages.

Deborah Clark
Partner at Mills & Reeve LLP
January 2024

Contents

Biography

Deborah Clark is a Partner at Mills & Reeve LLP, Solicitors. She specialises in private client work, advising clients on all aspects of estate planning and wealth protection. Deborah is recognised as being an expert on FICs, having been advising on the design and use of them for estate planning purposes for over a decade. Deborah is recognised as a ranked individual in *Chambers & Partners*. She regularly lectures on the use and design of FICs and is a Barrister, Chartered Tax Adviser and TEP.

Steve Collings FMAAT FCCA is the audit and technical partner at Leavitt Walmsley Associates Ltd where he trained and qualified. Steve specialises in auditing and financial reporting (UK GAAP and IFRS) and Solicitors Accounts Rules as well as having an interest in taxation issues for small and medium-sized businesses.

Adam Cooper is a Director – Tax Valuations at Mazars. He advises privately-owned businesses, private equity investors and management teams and on the efficient design and valuation of management incentive plans. He liaises with key stakeholders, tax advisors and lawyers to ensure plans effectively reward, incentivise and retain management teams, providing robust tax valuation advice consistent with the requirements of the relevant tax authorities.

Chapter 1

Introduction

1.1 Family Investment Companies (FICs) have become a popular estate planning vehicle for UK resident and domiciled individuals. Their main attraction is that they provide a vehicle into which family wealth can be invested and grown, ownership can be passed on to next generations, whilst control over the funds can be maintained. The rise in corporate tax rates have reduced their tax efficiency but they still offer tax savings if appropriately structured and managed.

However, whilst the focus for using a FIC is typically the tax benefits they offer, there is another key advantage the structure provides, that is governance. The creation of a FIC for a family is often the catalyst for valuable conversations around the meaning of family wealth, how it is to be preserved, what rights family members have to the benefits it provides and what role they have to manage or protect the wealth. It provides a framework in which information can be shared, expectations clarified and succession of control managed.

1.2 One of the first things to understand about FICs is that they are in many ways nothing special. We are just talking about a company, for the purposes of this book, a company registered in England and Wales at Companies House and resident in the UK for tax purposes. What makes a company a FIC, is that ownership of the company is generally shared between family members and the purpose of the company is to invest family wealth.

1.3 For example, a basic FIC used for estate planning could look like this:

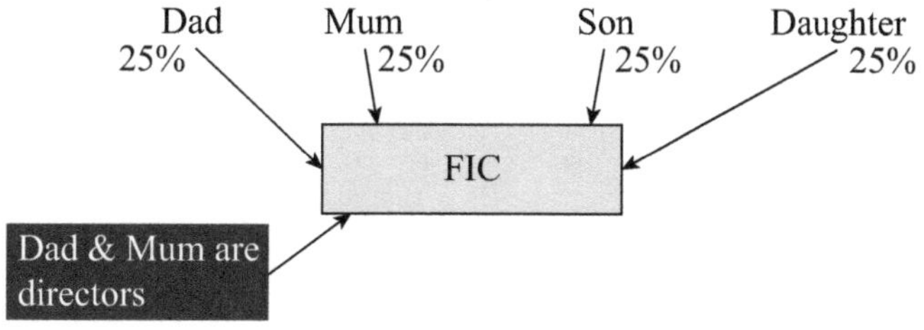

1.4 In this example, Mum and Dad have formed a FIC and given away half the company to their children. If established with cash and the shares are given away on incorporation, no tax will have arisen. The advantages of the FIC are:

- The gift by Mum and Dad of half the company will fall out of their estates after seven years, reducing their inheritance tax.
- Half the growth will belong to the children, saving further inheritance tax.
- Each of the children own minority interests which will have a discounted value in their estates for inheritance tax purposes, saving more tax.
- Mum and Dad only have a 50% interest in their estates for inheritance tax purposes which should also get a discount, saving them inheritance tax.
- Mum and Dad are both directors and they have all the day-to-day control of the FIC.
- The FIC invests the capital provided by Mum and Dad and the growth will only be taxed at corporation tax rates.
- Additional tax will be payable when profits are distributed but the timing and quantum of those distributions can be controlled by Mum and Dad.

Overall this structure works very well to reduce inheritance tax, grow the family wealth in a tax efficient vehicle and enable Mum and Dad to retain control over the funds.

1.5 When establishing a FIC there is no reason why a family, such as in the above example, cannot simply use a basic form of a company but to do so misses out on opportunities to create a structure that offers greater control, protection, flexibility and tax efficiency.

Chapter 2

Estate Planning Benefits

2.1 As highlighted throughout this book a FIC can assist in a number of ways with estate planning, including:

- Governance of family assets
- Managing succession
- Saving inheritance tax
- Protecting capital

GOVERNANCE

2.2 Creating a FIC provides a structure in which family wealth can be held and this provides an important framework for governance by:

- Establishing a decision making system;
- Producing financial records;
- Sharing information through board meetings and/or shareholder meetings;
- Establishing rules on ownership and participation; and
- Providing clarity around family expectations.

INHERITANCE TAX SAVING

2.3 The inheritance tax benefits come from a number of key sources:

- The reduction of the estate for the founders of the FIC. They will generally make a gift on formation of the company, by passing shares or cash for the subscription of shares, or loans to children/grandchildren. These initial gifts will be potentially exempt transfers and will save inheritance tax completely if the donor survives seven years. Often cash (used to subscribe for shares, or to be lent to the FIC) or shares are gifted to a family discretionary settlement. Such gifts will be chargeable lifetime transfers and therefore are typically restricted to the donor's available nil rate band if the 20% entry charge is to be avoided. After seven complete years, the donor's nil rate band will be refreshed.

- To the extent shares or debt are held by family members and not the founders, the profits generated by the FIC, either through share capital or loaned funds, will be outside the founders' estate, saving further inheritance tax.
- A material long term benefit comes from the way shares are valued. If a family member has a minority interest in the company, their shares are likely to attract a discount to reflect the size of interest. Discounts for investment companies are not the same as for trading companies but can still be advantageous. The cumulative effect of the discounts when looking at a family as a whole, can add up to a significant value and that value is not then subject to inheritance tax.
- A FIC is not within the relevant property regime so is not subject to ten-year anniversary charges of 6% like a new trust would be, or subject to exit charges.

MANAGING SUCCESSION

2.4 A FIC creates a vehicle which enables one generation to pass on wealth to the next in a controlled manner. This encourages passing on wealth sooner than later but also the structure provides a framework to introduce the next generation to the role of managing and looking after family wealth. The education process for the next generation often starts by involvement as a shareholder but can naturally develop into roles in the business, perhaps as part of an investment committee and ultimately to control as a director. The nature of the FIC provides the structure for managing the succession of both wealth and ultimately control.

PROTECTING CAPITAL

2.5 A FIC protects capital in a number of ways:

- Capital is controlled by the directors which protects against mis-management;
- Share capital is not easily extracted, which helps to ensure it is preserved for future generations; and
- The constitution of the FIC can help to protect against the impact of divorce by encouraging the use of marital agreements and by controlling the ownership of shares.

Chapter 3

Articles of Association

3.1 Every company must have articles of association. The articles set out the rules that the company officers must follow when running the company. They are the 'rule book' of the company. 'Model' articles of association are the standard default articles a limited company can use. They are prescribed by *The Companies (Model Articles) Regulations 2008*. When incorporating a limited company, you can choose to adopt the Model articles or a bespoke set of articles.

3.2 FICs are private companies with a share capital but they can be either limited or unlimited. The merits of the two forms of company are considered in Chapter 17. If a limited company is chosen the Model articles can be used but there are no model articles for an unlimited company.

3.3 When drafting articles for a limited company, many lawyers adopt the approach of drafting only the provisions that differ from the Model articles and then cross referring to the Model articles for the more standard and boiler plate provisions. This often produces a shorter form of articles but can be confusing, especially if you are not very familiar with Model articles.

3.4 The alternative approach is to use a long form set of articles that include all the rules relating to the company. This is often preferable for limited companies and is the only approach for unlimited companies.

The contents list of a standard set of articles will include five key parts, namely:

Part 1: Interpretation and limitation of liability.

Part 2: Directors, including directors' powers and responsibilities, decision-making by directors and appointment of directors.

Part 3: Shares and distributions.

Part 4: Decision-making by shareholders.

Part 5: Administrative arrangements.

3.5 When considering the rules that should be applied to a FIC, careful consideration of Parts 2, 3 and 4 are in particular required.

Chapter 4

Directors

4.1 All companies require at least one director, although it is always better to have more than one to reduce the risk of having no directors in place to run the company. There is no longer a requirement to have a company secretary. The directors of a company have extensive powers and are responsible for all the day-to-day operation of the company. Their powers come from the articles and are subject to the Companies Act.

4.2 The first directors are appointed on incorporation, and typically in a FIC, the first directors will be the founders. Once the first directors are appointed, they can have the power under the articles to appoint additional directors.

Under the Companies Act, the general duties of all directors are to:

- act within powers;
- promote the success of the Company;
- exercise independent judgement;
- exercise reasonable skill, care and diligence;
- avoid conflicts of interest;
- not accept benefits from third parties, and
- declare interests in proposed, existing transactions or arrangements with the company.

4.3 Directors will be responsible for running the company which means they will make all the decisions on how the FIC invests its funds, when to buy or sell assets, when to borrow or make loans (apart from loans to directors) and who to employ. The directors can also have sole control over the payment of interim dividends if the articles permit this.

4.4 It is important in the context of a FIC, to understand just how extensive directors' powers are and what decisions require shareholder approval as the issue of control is always a key concern for any family. It is often perceived, that where control is important, it is essential to retain voting control at shareholder level, but a more careful consideration of how a company is controlled reveals this may not be strictly necessary.

4.5 Directors only have to seek shareholder approval for a limited number of decisions. These include:

Ordinary resolutions:

(i) Substantial property transaction with a director;
(ii) Approving loans to directors;
(iii) Approving a share allotment;
(iv) Subdividing shares.

Special resolutions:

(i) Changing the Articles of Association;
(ii) Change of name;
(iii) Converting to Limited or Unlimited;
(iv) Reduction of share capital, purchase of own shares;
(v) Variation of class rights (by shareholders in that class).

4.6 Shareholders approve matters by either a special or an ordinary resolution. A special resolution requires 75% approval, an ordinary resolution requires more than 50% approval. Any single shareholder with 25% or less of the votes, is not capable of making or blocking decisions on their own.

4.7 If everyone has 25% or less, then co-operation is needed within the family for decisions to be made, a bit like everyone being a trustee, albeit that a majority decision is all that is likely to be needed. Returning to our simple example, if Mum, Dad, Son and Daughter all have 25% of the votes, any three of them will be required to pass a shareholder resolution. The Son and Daughter on their own, have no control or ability to block any decision.

4.8 Considering the list of what type of action the directors need to seek shareholder approval for, it is largely just matters relating to the structure of the company. It is not likely that a FIC will want to amend its share capital frequently, if at all, so it is worth considering if it really matters if adult children have to be consulted on such changes. An alternative view, is that it is actually important that all children are consulted on material changes to the FIC structure and that this helps to encourage engagement with the FIC which is a necessary element of managing the succession of control.

4.9 Under the Model Articles, the shareholders can appoint board members with just an ordinary resolution and this is a power that may be worth limiting, either in the articles or a supporting shareholders agreement. The shareholders also have an absolute power to remove a director with an ordinary resolution, and this power cannot be limited in the articles, so a shareholders' agreement is needed if you wish to restrict the power. Under a shareholders' agreement, the shareholders can agree to only exercise their powers to appoint or dismiss a director with the existing directors' consent. In the normal course of running a company, the directors will appoint and dismiss directors.

4.10 A consideration particularly relevant for a FIC, is what would happen if the board were wiped out in a family accident. In those circumstances, the shareholders would have to appoint the new directors, but this may be undesirable if the children are the other shareholders. It may therefore be helpful to make provisions for another shareholder, such as a family trust, or the personal representatives of the parents, to have special powers to appoint new directors. The founders can then ensure that suitable nominations are made for their successors.

4.11 The role of a director is an important one in any company but especially in a FIC and therefore families should give thought to who in the next generation will take on the role. It is important for the senior generation to see their role as helping the next generation to be well placed to take on the responsibility of running the family wealth. Providing experience and training becomes essential and a FIC provides a really helpful vehicle to do that, as it allows the next generation to start to become involved in the decision-making processes, first as shareholders and then later as directors. Managing the succession of control is as important as managing the succession of the wealth and in the authors view warrants as much planning.

Chapter 5

Share Capital

5.1 Shares are just a bundle of rights and these rights can be broken down into three types, namely:

1. voting;
2. income, and
3. capital.

5.2 To the non-corporate lawyer it is perhaps odd that the Model articles make no mention of share rights. This is because of the assumption that each share will have any equal right to participate in the company, which means an equal right to vote, income and capital. Where it is desirable for shares to have different rights, then those rights must be set out in the articles.

VOTING RIGHTS

5.3 Having a right to vote is a key part of being a shareholder and is likely to encourage shareholders to engage with the FIC much more than a shareholder with no right to vote. Encouraging engagement is important if the next generation are going to be ready to take over responsibility for the FIC.

5.4 Votes are exercised either at a shareholders' meeting or by approving a written resolution. How shareholders' meetings are run is set out in the articles of the company. Typically, at a shareholders' meeting, decisions are either taken on a show of hands or by a poll. A poll is where account is taken of how many votes each shareholder has. Any shareholder can normally ask for a decision to be made by way of a poll. As previously noted, decisions are either made by ordinary resolution, requiring over 50% of the votes, or by special resolution, requiring 75% or more of the votes. The Companies Act sets out what type of resolution is needed for certain decisions.

5.5 In this example, each family member just has 20% of the votes.

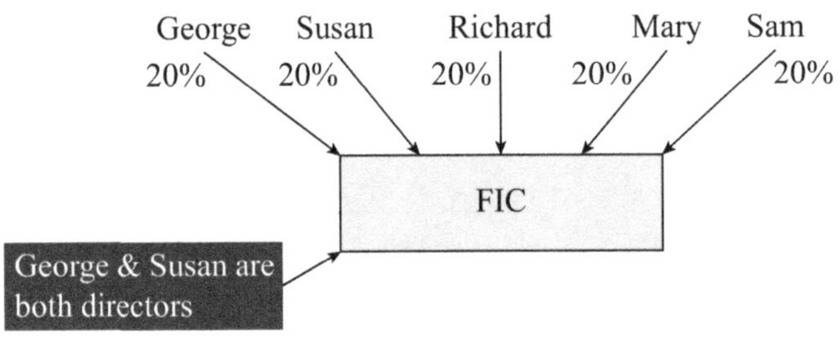

No one individual will have absolute control or be able to block any matter. If Sam disagreed with any matter he may become a nuisance but he cannot influence the running of the FIC or demand distributions (assuming everyone else is acting within their powers and appropriately). The position of a minority shareholder is much like a beneficiary of a discretionary trust. The other members of the family can make any decision that may be needed by shareholders, only three of them are needed to pass an ordinary resolution. Generally the family are encouraged to work together and for nearly all decisions they will be reliant on George and Susan as the directors who will be running the company and who will set the agenda for any shareholders' meetings.

5.6 Whilst encouraging engagement and co-operation is a good thing, it is understandable that some people still prefer to retain all the voting power in a company to have absolute control. In the above example, if George and Susan are the parents who provided all the funds for the company, they may want to retain total control. For that reason, they want to adopt an approach where their FIC will have a special class of shares that have all the voting rights, but no right to income or capital. This approach may be attractive but it does create its own issues.

5.7 First, shares with voting rights will have a material value. What that value is depends on the facts of the case but HM Revenue and Customs (HMRC) have been known to argue that shares that carried 100% of the voting rights in a FIC, had a value equivalent to 25% of the total value of the company. This stance may of course be challenged but HMRC's position seems clear, voting rights do have a significant value.

5.8 The second issue, comes from the very existence of these voting shares. What happens when George and Susan die, who exercises the control? In many cases, this issue is addressed by placing the shares in a discretionary trust but if the shares do have a significant value, this may create unwelcome tax charges when the trust reaches a ten-year anniversary under the relevant property regime. It also raises the issue of who will be the trustees of this trust. If George and Susan trust Richard and Mary but not Sam and make them the trustees, the position is much the same as if they all had voting shares in the first place, as Sam on his own couldn't do anything in any event.

5.9 There is of course no right or wrong answer to how control is managed or whether or not all or just some shares should have voting rights, but any decision should of course be made having considered all of the issues.

INCOME RIGHTS

5.10 A company distributes its profits (made up of its income and gains) to its shareholders in the form of dividends. The right to a dividend, is referred to as the income rights of a shareholder. The right to participate in the profits of a company is another key part of being a shareholder.

5.11 It is possible to give some shares a special right to income, such as a right to be paid first before other shares get a dividend, or a right to a fixed level of income. Such shares are generally called 'preference shares' (although the preferential terms may be to income and/or capital). A FIC may want to issue preference shares to a family member that has a particular need for income. However, in most cases it is preferable to retain discretion so preference shares are not often used in FICs to give preferential rights to income.

5.12 Where the directors retain discretion over the timing and amount of dividends paid to shareholders they will often also want to be able to pay different dividends to different shareholders. The ability to do this is generally achieved by using alphabet shares. The term, 'alphabet shares' just means shares that are of a different class. For ease of naming, each class of share is given a different letter of the alphabet, such as Ordinary A Shares, Ordinary B Shares and Ordinary C Shares.

5.13 By creating different classes of shares, all of which generally have an equal right to income, the directors can declare different dividends on each class of share. For example, George and Susan's company has issued different share classes to each of the five shareholders who each have a 20% entitlement to the income. The company has made a £50,000 profit.

Shareholder	**Class of Shares**	**20% Equal share of profit**	**Dividend declared**
George	Ordinary A	£10,000	£0
Susan	Ordinary B	£10,000	£0
Richard	Ordinary C	£10,000	£10,000
Mary	Ordinary D	£10,000	£10,000
Sam	Ordinary E	£10,000	£2,000
Total		£50,000	£22,000

By creating different share classes, George and Susan as directors can decide what dividend to pay to each shareholder. In the above case, they have decided that they do not want any dividend,

Richard and Mary would benefit from their full entitlement but Sam only needs a small dividend of £2,000. If everyone had the same class of shares, George and Susan, as directors would not be able to achieve the above unless they and Sam agreed to waive their entitlement to dividends. Whilst they may be happy to do that, they are unlikely to want to leave that decision with Sam.

5.14 When using alphabet shares care needs to be taken if distributions are made to a shareholder above their entitlement. The concern lies in the potential application of the Settlements Legislation found in the *Income Tax (Trading and Other Income) Act 2005* (*ITTOIA 2005), Pt 5, Ch 5*. The legislation seeks to prevent the avoidance of tax by individuals who direct their income to someone who will pay tax at a lower rate than they would. For example say, George and Susan want to have a dividend of £20,000 but George will pay tax at the additional rate of 39.35% on his dividend, whereas Susan will only pay at the basic rate of 8.75%. George and Susan could decide to pay a dividend of £20,000 to Susan and for George not to take any dividend. Under the Settlements Legislation, HMRC may challenge the position and argue that £10,000 of Susan's dividend belongs to George and should be taxed on him. This issue is considered further at Chapter 12.

5.15 One possible solution to the risk of challenge under the Settlements Legislation, is to limit the rights attaching to each class of shares so that they can only receive dividends up to their proportionate share in the distributable reserves. If a dividend is not paid up to their full entitlement, the shares retain the right to those reserves. Such restrictions can be included in the articles of association. It does add complication to the articles and when issuing new shares, but can also be a useful way of ensuring that all shareholders are treated equally. In the following example, the entitlement to the profits is ring fenced for each class of shares, so to the extent their share of profit is not distributed, they retain the entitlement to the profits going forward.

Share class	Percentage entitlement	Share of profits	Dividend paid	Entitlement carried forward
Ordinary A shares	40%	£4,000	£4,000	£0
Ordinary B shares	35%	£3,500	£2,000	£1,500
Ordinary C shares	25%	£2,500	0	£2,500
Total	100%	£10,000	£6,000	£4,000

5.16 Limiting dividend rights may also address any concerns that parents have a reservation of benefit in shares gifted to children resulting in the value of the shares remaining in the parents' estates for inheritance tax purposes. For example, in the above example, if George and Susan retained the right, by virtue of being directors, to pay all the income generated by the company to themselves by paying higher dividends on their A and B shares, to the detriment of the children's, C, D and E shares, it may be suggested that they retained a benefit in the C, D and E shares. If, under the articles, George and Susan can never benefit from the income entitlement of the C, D and E shares, such an argument would not be possible.

5.17 One final note on creating different share classes is that it is necessary to ensure that each share class has slightly different rights. Giving shares a different name is not itself sufficient to create a different class of shares if the share rights are all identical.

CAPITAL RIGHTS

5.18 The final key right of a shareholder, is their right to capital, which may arise on a winding up or other capital distribution. Often the entitlement to capital will also apply on a sale of the entire share capital of the company.

5.19 The default position is that all shares will have an equal right to capital but it is possible to give some shares a different entitlement, such as a right to be paid capital ahead of other share classes, such shares can also be called preference shares. An alternative approach is to give some shares a right to future growth ahead of other shares and these shares are often called 'growth shares'.

5.20 The concept of a growth share is that it is a share that has a low value when issued but acquires more value over time. Having a low initial value means the share can be gifted to other individuals without triggering a material gain that will result in a capital gains tax charge.

5.21 Growth shares can be useful in the context of FICs, especially where the FIC already has valuable assets. For example, Richard established an investment company many years ago, and over time has built a valuable portfolio of investment properties. His shares in the company are now worth £100 each, and his base cost is just the original subscription price of £1.00. If Richard gives any shares to his daughter, Sally, the gift will be a disposal for capital gains tax purposes and will trigger a £99 gain per share on which Richard will have to pay capital gains tax. An alternative approach for Richard, is to subdivide his shares so that he has one Ordinary Share and one Growth Share. The Ordinary Share's entitlement to capital will be capped, to a value that is equivalent to the current value of the share plus an appropriate hurdle (say 20% in this example), which would be £120 per share. Once the value exceeds the cap of 120% of the current value, future growth will belong to the Growth Share. The purpose of the hurdle is to ensure that the Growth Share has a low current value, as the company still has to grow in value by a further 20% before any value passes into the Growth Share. Given the Growth Shares will have a low value, Richard can give these shares to Sally, without triggering a material capital gain. If undertaking planning with growth shares, specialist share valuation advice should be taken to ensure that the value of the growth share is correctly assessed.

Chapter 6

Share Transfers

6.1 Model articles of association say little on share transfers, other than:

- transfers are made by an instrument in the usual form;
- the transferor remains the shareholder until the transfer is recorded in the register of members;
- the company should not charge a fee for registering a transfer; and
- directors can refuse to register a transfer.

6.2 Including more bespoke share transfer provisions will be appropriate for nearly all FICs.

6.3 One approach may be to simply state that board approval is needed for all share transfers. This would give the directors discretion but, in the absence of more detailed guidance, it leaves open challenges on how the discretion should be applied. It is therefore much better to set out guidelines of what transfers will be permitted and perhaps more importantly what will not.

6.4 The permitted transfers that may be appropriate for a FIC, are transfers to:

- family members; and
- trusts for family members.

6.5 What is meant by 'Family' should of course be defined carefully given the potential for blended families. Typically lineal descendants of the founders may be an appropriate starting point but this may be deemed too narrow by some. Parents are also likely to be concerned about the impact of a divorce in the family and therefore expressly excluding spouses and civil partners from being shareholders will be an important consideration.

6.6 The desire to exclude spouses and civil partners can of course conflict with other planning. For example, what happens when a shareholder dies leaving a surviving spouse. In this situation it may be appropriate to extend the definition of a family trust to include trusts established in a Will on the death of a shareholder giving the surviving spouse a life interest. This will secure spouse relief, avoiding an inheritance tax charge on the value of the shares. The trustees of such a trust can be given instructions to ensure that the shares come back to family members either on the death of the surviving spouse or earlier. Using a trust is preferable to leaving the shares absolutely to the surviving spouse as it may then be more difficult to control what happens to the shares after the death of the surviving spouse, although the general compulsory transfer provisions referred to below would assist.

6.7 Trustees will have the right to exercise the voting rights of shares held by the family trust, so it is appropriate that the board have some ability to approve the trustees. Whilst the directors could not directly force a change of trustees in a family trust, they can control who is entered on the register of members, so can exclude a trustee from being a member of the company, preventing them from having direct voting rights and discouraging the appointment of a undesirable trustee.

6.8 In addition to permitted transfers, provisions may also be included in the articles to deal with the compulsory transfer of shares on certain events, such as death, bankruptcy and/or divorce. Compulsory transfer provisions may also apply if a shareholder is in breach of any rules, for example, the shares being left in a Will to someone not permitted to be a shareholder.

6.9 The board is typically given the power to determine when and if they wish to trigger the compulsory transfer provisions. If they do, the board can determine what happens to the shares. Options may include:

- the company could buy the shares back (if permitted to do so and it has the distributable reserves);
- another family member or family trust may purchase the shares, or
- the shares may be offered around the other shareholders.

6.10 The articles would normally include details of the process for implementing the compulsory transfer provisions and would include a procedure for agreeing the price to be paid for the shares being compulsory purchased. The basis for valuing the shares may also be included in the articles and normally this would be the open market value taking account of the size of holding.

Chapter 7

Valuation Issues for Family Investment Companies

7.1 Transactions between family members and a family investment company can trigger various tax charges. A valuation may be required to determine the amount that is subject to tax. These transactions include:

- **A subscription for share or loan capital in the company** – If the subscription does not take place at market value there could be a transfer of value from the existing shareholders to the new shareholder (or vice versa). This may be treated as a chargeable lifetime transfer.
- **A gift of share or loan capital in the company to a family member** – For capital gains tax purposes the gift could be deemed to have taken place at market value. This may crystallise a capital gain (or loss) for the donor. Gifts to certain trusts could also be treated as a chargeable lifetime transfer.
- **A transfer of assets to the company** – If the transferor does not receive consideration equal to the market value of the assets transferred, then the reduction in the value of the transferor's estate could be treated as a chargeable lifetime transfer. Depending on the type of asset, stamp duty or stamp duty land tax could also be payable by the company.

In each case market value is the key to assessing possible tax consequences.

BASIS OF VALUE

7.2 For both inheritance tax and capital gains tax, the relevant basis of value is 'market value'. This is defined in statute as follows:[1]

> '… the price which those assets might reasonably be expected to fetch if sold in the open market …'

For unquoted shares and securities the following must also be considered:

> '… it shall be assumed that … there is available to any prospective purchaser … all the information which a prudent prospective purchaser of the asset might reasonably require if he were proposing to purchase it from a willing vendor by private treaty and at arm's length.'

[1] *IHTA 1984, s 160* (for inheritance tax) and *TCGA 1992, s 272* (for capital gains tax).

In addition to these statutory provisions there is a wide body of case law which has established several key principles. This includes the requirement to assume that the open market is totally unrestricted from which no potential purchaser is excluded. Any restrictions in the Articles of Association or a shareholders' agreement are ignored when establishing the pool of prospective purchasers[2]. The valuation should therefore take into consideration the rights that could be exercised by a third-party purchaser and how the actions of other shareholders may change in response to a non-family shareholder acquiring the shares.

LOSS TO DONOR

7.3 Where a gift is made by a family member, any charge to inheritance tax is calculated by reference to the fall in value of the donor's estate. This can differ from the market value of the gift in isolation.

For example, suppose a company has 1,000 ordinary shares in issue. The father owns 600 shares and each of his two sons own 200 shares. The father transfers 200 shares to one of his sons.

For inheritance tax purposes we consider the value of his estate before and after the transfer. Prior to the transfer the father held a majority shareholding but after the transfer he holds a minority shareholding. He has lost control of the company and therefore the reduction in the value of his estate may be substantially higher than the value of 200 shares in isolation.

RELATED PROPERTY

7.4 When valuing the assets in an estate for inheritance tax purposes, related property is aggregated. Related property includes any assets in the estate of the person's spouse or civil partner.

For example, suppose a company has 1,000 ordinary shares in issue. The husband owns 400 shares, the wife owns 400 shares and their two children own 100 shares each. The husband gifts 400 shares to his children. Together, the husband and wife held 800 shares which is a controlling shareholding. Under the related property rules, the husband's shares are valued as though they form half of an 800-share controlling shareholding. This gives a higher value than if they were valued in isolation as a 400-share minority shareholding (which would reflect a minority discount).

[2] Though the price a prospective purchaser would be prepared to pay should reflect the impact of those restrictions.

VALUING SHAREHOLDINGS IN A FAMILY INVESTMENT COMPANY

7.5 Shareholdings in a family investment company can be valued as follows:

- Indirectly, by estimating the total value of the company and calculating the proportion of total value which should be allocated to the subject shareholding. This is typically the preferred approach for control shareholdings or where a capital return is most likely. This is discussed further at **7.6** (Valuing investment companies) and **7.9** (Allocation of total value).
- Directly, by estimating the value of the shareholding based on the income the holder expects to receive. This is typically the preferred approach for minority shareholdings in dividend paying companies. This is discussed further at **7.11** (Dividend yield methodology).

It may be that both approaches should be used.

VALUING INVESTMENT COMPANIES

7.6 Investment companies are often valued using an asset-based valuation methodology. This involves estimating the market value of the company's assets and deducting the market value of its liabilities. This methodology cannot be used for companies with trading activity which may hold intangible assets or goodwill not recognised on the company's balance sheet.

The book value of the assets and liabilities may be a good starting point, but adjustments may be required where book values are not representative of market value.

7.7 Whether it is necessary to revalue a company's assets and liabilities will depend on the accounting policy, whether the asset or liability represents a large or small proportion of total company value and the length of time since the last balance sheet date. For example, no adjustment may be required if the asset or liability is fair valued at each balance sheet date and there has been no material change in circumstances since that date. Conversely, a valuation may be required if an asset or liability is recorded at historical cost and it represents a large proportion of total company value.

7.8 An appropriate valuation methodology for each of the company's assets and liabilities will depend on the category of asset or liability. Some examples include:

- **Investment in a trading subsidiary** – A valuation of that trading subsidiary may be required (using a multiple of earnings or a discounted cash flow methodology) to calculate the market value of the company's shareholding.
- **Commercial property** – The property could be valued by reference to its rental income, taking into consideration rent reviews under the terms of the lease, the creditworthiness of

the tenant (and other potential tenants in the market) and alternatives for more profitable uses. The valuation principles are set out by the Royal Institute of Chartered Surveyors (RICS),

- **Loan** – If the company has made/received a loan, its market value may differ from its face value. The market value of a loan is calculated by discounting the future interest and principal receipts/payments to present value at a market (or commercial) rate of interest. This is discussed further at **7.23** (Valuing other fixed income securities).

Further adjustments may be required in respect of unrealised chargeable gains which would become taxable if the assets were disposed of. Such adjustments are only typical in respect of interests in properties and should take account of the fact that the tax would not be immediately payable.

ALLOCATION OF TOTAL VALUE

7.9 A common methodology for allocating the total value of a company across its shares is to calculate the proceeds each shareholder would receive on an immediate sale or liquidation. This will depend on the capital rights set out in the company's Articles of Association. In the context of investment companies this is often referred to as their 'liquidation value' and is most appropriate where a sale or liquidation is expected, or the company only has a single class of share.

7.10 For companies with more complex share capital structures where a sale or liquidation is not expected, this methodology may not be appropriate. For example:

- The market value of preference shares may not equate to their liquidation value (being their face value plus any accrued but unpaid dividends[3]). If the preference dividend is above a market rate, over time the holder is generating a higher return on their investment than the risk they are taking, and the market value of the preference shares will be higher than their liquidation value (and vice versa). The market value of the ordinary shares should be calculating by deducting the market value of the preference shares from the total value of the company. More details are set out at **7.18** (Valuing preference shares).
- Growth shares have no liquidation value where the threshold for them receiving returns exceeds the current value of the company. However, it is well established that growth shares have some market value where there is a possibility that the value of the company could exceed the hurdle in the future. The market value of growth shares must be estimated using the methods set out at **7.27** (Valuing growth shares).

[3] Assuming the value of the company's assets are sufficient to fully repay the face value plus accrued dividend.

DIVIDEND YIELD METHODOLOGY

7.11 As minority shareholders cannot influence the timing or quantum of income or capital returns, a dividend yield methodology is often used to value minority shareholdings. This involves dividing a maintainable dividend by a required dividend yield.

7.12 This methodology is more appropriate for companies that pay regular dividends and have a stable level of earnings. However, in practice, dividends will often vary from year to year depending on the income generated from the company's investments and the personal circumstances of the controlling shareholder.

7.13 Where the controlling shareholders' circumstances are such that they do not require the payment of dividends, the company's profits may be reinvested. This means there is no clear route to a return for a minority shareholder. One approach is to estimate the market value of the shares based on a notional dividend the company could afford to pay and then apply a significant discount for non-payment.

7.14 A key consideration in relation to this methodology is a company's dividend cover. This is the number of times the dividend could be paid out of current net profit. This is calculated by dividing the company's net profit by the dividend paid and is usually a number greater than one. The greater the dividend cover the more secure the dividend is. A company with a high dividend cover may be able to maintain the current level of dividend even if there is a decline in profitability and may be able to increase it in the future.

7.15 A dividend yield is typically estimated based on the divided yields of quoted comparable companies and is calculated by dividing dividends paid by the company's share price. An uplift to the dividend yield should be made to reflect the fact that, compared to a quoted company, there is not a ready market for shares in a family held private company. Adjustments should also be made for other differences between the company and the quoted comparable companies. For example, size and diversity, sector and geographical focus, dividend policy and dividend cover.

MINORITY DISCOUNTS

7.16 When valuing a minority shareholding in a private company for tax purposes, it is well established that significant discounts should be applied to reflect the lack of control conferred by such minority shareholdings. Votes are a means of unlocking the value of a company by declaring dividends or liquidating the company. The absence of votes can be a significant depreciatory factor. The following factors are relevant when assessing the quantum of the discount:

- **Size of the shareholding** – A minority shareholding conferring greater than 25% of the votes could block a special resolution whereas a shareholding conferring 25% of the votes or fewer could not.

- **Spread of shares** – Minority shareholdings are more influential where there is no single controlling shareholder. Cooperation between minority shareholders could enable them to pass or block ordinary and special resolutions.
- **Dividend policy** – If the company is already paying out all its profits as dividends, a controlling shareholder could not increase these. An inability to sell the shares is also less important because the minority shareholder is receiving an income return on its shares. Conversely, if all profits are reinvested and the controlling shareholder has no intention to liquidate the company, the route to a return would seem remote and a significant discount should be applied.
- **Minority protections** – The directors cannot unfairly prejudice minority shareholders which provides some degree of protection. Additional protections may also be included within the company's Articles of Association or shareholders' agreement.
- **Transfer provisions for the shares** – If the Articles of Association only permit transfers to other family members, then the shares are even less marketable.

HMRC used to publish minority discounts for different shareholding percentages in the Shares & Assets Valuation Manual but this was withdrawn several years ago. HMRC were concerned that the discounts were being blindly adopted as representing a standard measure. An appropriate discount will depend on the facts of each case.

7.17 Case law can be useful where there is a close resemblance to the facts of a particular case. Cases of interest include:

- *Battle v IRC* [1980] STC 86 – This concerned the valuation of two 49% shareholdings in an investment company where a 12.5% discount was applied; and
- *Executors of MacArthur (deceased) v Revenue and Customs Commissioners* SpC 700; [2008] STC (SCD) 1100 – This concerned the valuation of various sized shareholdings in moneybox companies which held a mixture of property and quoted stocks and shares[4].

However, HMRC has stated that the case law does not provide a set of rules of thumb which can be applied elsewhere without close study of the facts of each decided case.

Various other methods have also been developed for quantifying discounts for lack of marketability and control including restricted stock studies, control premium studies and put option modelling.

VALUING PREFERENCE SHARES

7.18 Preference shares are a class of share which rank in priority to other share classes with regards to income and/or capital. The rights of preference shares can vary, but the holder is typically entitled to the face value in priority to other share classes on a winding up (but not any surplus). Preference shares usually also carry a fixed right to dividends.

[4] A 12.5% discount for 51.1% and 69.9% shareholdings, a 45% discount for a 26.8% shareholding and a 65% discount for a 8.16% shareholding.

7.19 Preference shares are normally valued by reference to their preference dividend. If the preference dividend represents a market (or commercial) rate of return the market value of the preference shares will equate to their face value. However, if the preference dividend is higher (or lower) than a market rate of return, over time the holder is generating a higher (or lower) return on their investment than the risk they are taking, and the market value of the preference shares will be higher (or lower) than their face value.

7.20 A market rate of return can be estimated from the yields available on quoted preference shares with a similar risk profile. Adjustments are often required for differences between:

- **The risk profiles of the companies** – The more stable a company's cash flows, the lower the risk of non-payment. Relevant factors include whether the company is a trading company or an investment company (and the risk profile of its investments), its exposure to geographical or sector specific risk and whether it generates its income from a diverse range of sources.
- **The seniority of the preference shares** – If the company has debt outstanding which ranks in priority to the preference shares, the risk of non-payment of dividends or capital is higher.
- **The face value of the preference shares as a proportion of company value** – The higher the proportion, the greater the risk there will be insufficient proceeds to fully redeem the preference shares if the value of the company's investments declines.
- **Marketability** – All else being equal, the value of quoted preference shares is higher than preference shares in a private company. However, where the preference shares are redeemable, marketability is less important (unless a sale of the preference shares would yield a higher return than a redemption).

Preference shares are valued using a discounted cash flow methodology. The preference dividends and redemption payment are projected over the period to the expected redemption date and are discounted to present value at the selected market rate of return.

7.21 Redemption rights impact the market value of preference shares. If the preference shareholder has the sole discretion to redeem the preference shares, their market value will be no less than the amount for which they could immediately be redeemed (even if the preference dividend is less than a market rate). Conversely, if the directors have the sole discretion to redeem the preference shares, their market value will be no more than the amount for which they could immediately be redeemed (even if the preference dividend is more than a market rate).

7.22 A common way of ensuring there is no transfer of value on the issuance of the preference shares is to give immediate redemption rights to both parties. Even if the preference shares do not pay a preference dividend, HMRC is likely to accept that the market value of the preference shares is equal to the amount for which they could be immediately redeemed. However, where the preference dividend is less than a market rate this could still be considered a bounteous arrangement under the settlements legislation if there is no intention to redeem those preference shares.

VALUING OTHER FIXED INCOME SECURITIES

7.23 Many of the concepts discussed in the context of preference shares also relate to loans. Loans are also valued by reference to the market rate of interest. Their market value is calculated by discounting the interest and principal payments to present value at a market rate of interest.

7.24 A market rate of interest is often expressed as a risk-free rate (usually calculated from the yields available on 'risk-free' investments such as government bonds) plus a credit spread to reflect the risk of non-payment of interest or principal. The credit spread can be sourced from the spreads on quoted corporate bonds with a similar risk profile or credit rating.

7.25 It should be noted that where a family investment company is established and funded entirely by way of a loan, a market rate of interest on that loan does not exist. It would not be possible for a company to secure a loan from a third party where no equity funding is being provided. The market value of the loan will be less than its face value and there will be a transfer of value from the lender to the shareholders[5].

7.26 The transfer of value into the shares can be estimated using the methodologies set out at **7.27** (Valuing growth shares). This is because highly leveraged equity is economically similar to a growth share. There are very few circumstances in which the value of shares in a company is nil.

VALUING GROWTH SHARES

7.27 Growth shares are a special class of share which are designed to only deliver a return if the value of the company increases above a pre-determined threshold. The threshold is usually set at a premium to the current value of the company, so the initial value of the growth shares is low.

7.28 For many years HMRC accepted that the market value of a growth share could be equated to its intrinsic or liquidation value. The intrinsic/liquidation value of a share is the proceeds the holder would receive on an immediate sale/liquidation of the company at its current value. Where the current value of the company was lower than the threshold HMRC accepted that growth shares had negligible market value.

7.29 However, several years ago HMRC changed its approach, and it is now well established that growth shares should be valued based on the expected future proceeds. This is not unreasonable since in most cases an immediate sale or liquidation of the company is highly unlikely and there is an expectation the value of the company will increase.

[5] If the loan is immediately repayable HMRC may accept that its market value is equal to the amount of the repayment. However, the loan could still be considered a bounteous arrangement under the settlements legislation.

7.30 When projecting the expected future proceeds, it is important to consider both the capital and income rights of the growth shares and which route to a return is most likely. Growth shares are often designed with different capital and income thresholds or a single threshold which is reduced by both capital and income distributions to other share classes. It is usually necessary to project both capital appreciation of the company's assets and its income distributions in order to calculate the timing and quantum of growth share proceeds.

7.31 The market value of a growth share is calculated by discounting the expected future proceeds to present value at a rate of return which reflects both the risk inherent in the company's investments and the risk associated with an investment in a class of shares which only delivers a return if a threshold is exceeded. An appropriate rate of return will be higher than the rate of return expected on the company's underlying investments since other shares rank in priority to growth shares.

7.32 In some cases, it will be necessary to consider multiple sets of projections and probability weight each case. This is because growth shares have significant upside potential but limited downside risk and this can only be reflected by using multiple sets of projections. This methodology is commonly referred to as a probability weighted expected returns model (or PWERM).

7.33 Where the most likely route to a return is a return of capital, growth shares can also be valued using an option pricing model (such as Black-Scholes). This is because the economic return on a growth share is similar to that of a share option. A growth share only delivers a return if the value of the company exceeds the threshold and a share option over delivers a return if the share price exceeds the exercise price.

VOTING ONLY SHARES

7.34 As discussed, a company's share capital can be structured so that one class of share confers all (or the majority) of the voting rights but none of the income and capital rights. Despite not sharing in the capital value of the company or the profits it generates, the market value of voting only shares can still be substantial.

7.35 An asset has value if the holder can turn it into cash or use it to generate cash, be that directly or indirectly. There are several reasons voting-only shares could confer value indirectly:

- Votes are a means of unlocking the company's income and capital value. Other shareholders without any voting rights might bid for the voting-only shares so they can increase their dividends or liquidate the company.

- Whomever controls the company can appoint and remove Directors (including appointing themselves) and Directors can be remunerated for their role at an above market rate[6]. The Directors can also decide how the company invests its funds, when to buy or sell assets and when to pay dividends.
- The shares could be the subject of a nuisance bid from a non-family member with competing business interests[7]. Whilst the *Companies Act 2006* includes a requirement not to unfairly prejudice minority shareholders, in practice a controlling shareholder could cause significant nuisance.

HMRC has been known to cite the New Zealand case of *Holt v Holt* [1990] 1 WLR 1250 when considering the value of voting only shares. This was a matrimonial case involving the value of one A share in a family company which owned a farm estate. The A share conferred the vast majority of the votes but a negligible portion of the assets of a winding up.

7.36 As the A share conferred voting control, the A shareholder could be appointed sole director. They could occupy the farm and run the estate as they see fit for as long as they like, drawing reasonable remuneration. The court likened this position to that of a tenant for life, impeachable for waste, with the additional benefit of being able to transfer the shares to another party (and thus create another tenant for life). In this case it was determined that 20% of the value of the company should be attributed to voting control.

7.37 The percentage of company value attributable to voting control will depend on the facts of each case. For example, where a family member has made a loan to the company which is repayable on demand, the family member could cause the company to be wound up by demanding repayment of the loan were an external investor to acquire voting control. This would limit the benefit of voting control.

7.38 The value of control may not necessarily be directly proportionate to the value of the company. In Holt v Holt 20% of the value of the value of the company was NZD150,000. For larger companies the value of control may represent a smaller proportion of company value if, for example, the benefit is limited to drawing directors' remuneration.

Even in cases where the voting only shares do not confer absolute control, there may still be an element of nuisance value.

[6] Though not so high as to enable other shareholders to bring about an unfair prejudice claim.
[7] As noted at **5.2** (Basis of value), any restrictions preventing the sale of the shares to non-family members are set aside for the purpose of determining the pool of prospective purchasers.

Chapter 8

Shareholders' Agreement

8.1 As noted, articles of association are the rule book for a company and where possible all the important rules that you want to apply to a FIC should be included within the articles. There are however two limitations to this:

1. First, the *Companies Act 2006* will in some cases override provisions in the articles where they are not compatible with the act.
2. Secondly, the articles are a public document and some matters are better kept private.

8.2 A shareholders' agreement is a very useful way to incorporate further rules on a FIC, which can't otherwise be included in the articles. It is generally drafted to be a legally binding contract between the shareholders and usually the company, whereby the parties agree on matters relating to the operation of the company. It is normally a private document.

8.3 A typical shareholders' agreement in a commercial context is used to limit the directors' powers without recourse to shareholders (recognising just how much power directors actually have). For example, the board of directors may be required to obtain shareholder approval before issuing more shares, making large investments, taking out loans or selling assets. Often referred to as 'reserved matters' the shareholders' agreement can limit the scope of the directors' powers.

8.4 In a FIC situation, a shareholders' agreement is used to the opposite effect, as its main purpose is for the shareholders to agree only to exercise their voting rights in situations where the directors need them to approve matters they have proposed. For example, the shareholders agree that they will only use their voting rights to amend the articles, issue shares or appoint directors with the board's prior approval to such action. This would prevent, for example, a group of shareholders proposing to take action that the board disagrees with.

8.5 Where a shareholders' agreement exists, the articles will generally make the signing of a deed of adherence to the shareholders' agreement a pre-condition before being entered into the register of members of a company. This ensures that new shareholders must agree to the terms of the shareholders' agreement. It can be a useful mechanism to ensure that anyone that becomes entitled to shares previously held in trust (including a bare trust) must become a party to the shareholders' agreement before they can become the legal owner of the shares.

8.6 A shareholders' agreement for a FIC may include:

- A statement setting out the purpose of the FIC, for example is it a vehicle to grow wealth for future generations or to provide financial support for current shareholders;
- Clarity around what information shareholders will be entitled to see and what level of engagement is expected;
- Details of the first directors and how they will be appointed going forward;
- Information on the dividend policy;
- Details of family expectations, will shareholders be expected to enter into pre-marital agreements and must they have a Will to ensure that the shares in the FIC are protected as much as possible;
- Undertakings not to use their shares as security for loans; and
- A process to resolve family disputes.

Chapter 9

Governance

9.1 There is no doubt that in practice, most private companies are run very successfully on a very informal basis. But the running of a company does require some formality, whether as a result of legislation, provisions in the articles of association or under a shareholders' agreement. Ensuring these formalities are complied with is good governance.

9.2 Complying with formalities may seem a burden, but should be viewed as an opportunity, especially to help with the financial education of the next generation. A successful FIC will be one where control is transferred from one generation to the next, ensuring that the capital continues to grow and provide a resource and potential source of income for family members for a number of generations. Managing the transfer of control requires both planning and training and that process is achieved by involving family members, whether as a director, a committee member or simply by attending an annual meeting as a shareholder.

DIRECTORS' MEETINGS

9.3 The articles of association set out the rules for who can call a directors' meeting, how much notification is required and who has to be present. The role of a chairman, is to ensure these rules are complied with. Failure to meet the requirements in the articles, may mean that decisions taken in that meeting are not binding.

9.4 Under the model articles applicable to a limited company, any director can call a directors' meeting and when they do, notice must be given to all directors of when, where and at what time, the meeting will be held. Notice does not need to be in writing and the notice period must be fair and reasonable. Directors can agree to hold meetings at short notice and if all the directors will not be in the same location, notice has to be given on how they will be able to communicate with each other during the meeting.

9.5 Decisions at board meetings are generally made by a simple majority subject to anything in the articles of association or shareholders' agreement which may add additional requirements for certain decisions.

9.6 Provided all directors agree, directors' meetings can be held informally and if it is difficult for directors to get together, they can make decisions by written resolution.

9.7 There is no legal requirement to hold a minimum number of directors' meeting but directors do need to bear in mind their obligations as directors and should meet as often as is necessary to carry out their duties properly. In relation to a family investment company, it is likely that the directors will all be family members and they may choose to operate informally, making decisions 'round the kitchen table'.

9.8 Minutes of decisions made by the directors must be taken (*Companies Act 2006, s 248(1)*). The model articles for limited companies states at Article 15:

> 'The directors must ensure that the company keeps a record, in writing, for at least 10 years from the date of the decision recorded, of every unanimous or majority decision taken by the directors.'

USE OF COMMITTEES

9.9 Directors are entitled to delegate matters to a committee that may include non-directors. Having a committee may be a useful way to involve adult children with the running of a FIC without giving them a formal role as a director. For example, the directors of a FIC may decide to have an 'Investment Committee' that will consider suitable investments and decide where to invest. Any member of the committee may propose investments to be considered.

SHAREHOLDER MEETINGS

9.10 The directors of the company will generally call a shareholders' meeting where they feel it is required. A shareholder with at least 5% of the voting rights can also require the directors to call a shareholders' meeting, and where such a request is made, the meeting should be called within 21 days and actually held within 28 days.

9.11 Private companies are not legally required to have an annual shareholder meeting but holding such meetings can be a useful way of involving all the family members. Holding meetings also gives the directors an opportunity to report back on the investment performance of the company and any decisions on the payment of dividends.

Chapter 10

Directors and Employees

10.1 All FICs will need to have at least one director. A company is not obliged to pay directors a fee for carrying out that role, but they can choose to do so. A director's fee will be treated in the same way as a salary for tax purposes so subject to PAYE and national insurance. Accordingly, the FIC will need to establish a payroll if directors fees are paid.

10.2 Just like any other company a FIC may also choose to employ people to carry out roles for the company. It goes without saying that any employment needs to have substance, it mustn't be a sham and all the normal obligations that come with employing individuals, such as adhering to minimum wages legislation, payroll responsibilities, pensions etc should be considered. For example, if the FIC has a large property portfolio it may employ someone to manage the properties. There is nothing preventing the FIC from employing family members to carry out such roles and this may be a useful way to involve the next generation in helping to manage family assets.

10.3 If a FIC is likely to employ family members it would be worthwhile to set out in the shareholders' agreement some guidelines on when a family member may be employed to ensure no family member acquires an unrealistic expectation or sense of entitlement that they will be offered employment.

10.4 Care does need to be taken if a family decide to rely on paying a salary or director's fee to a family member to provide them with an income from the FIC. If the individual is a director, they may receive a director's fee for carrying out that role, but an elderly relative that has lost mental capacity cannot be a director, so they will lose their right to a directors' fee. If the individual is an employee, there must be a genuine role that they carry out. Again, an elderly relative may not be able to perform the duties of an employment contract, so cannot rely on the salary as a source of income for life.

10.5 When considering what level of salary or director's fee to pay, care needs to be taken to ensure that the amount is commensurate with the duties performed. This is important for the FIC to be able to claim a tax deduction for the payments made. But it is also especially important for the founders of the FIC who will have given shares to family members. The reservation of benefit rules were introduced in the *Finance Act 1986* (*FA 1986, s 102(2)*) to prevent individuals giving assets away and continuing to benefit from them. These rules may be brought into play if the founders, who have given shares to family members, then proceed to pay themselves inflated salaries or directors' fees. The concern is that such situations can be argued as creating a reservation of benefit as the founders retained the right to determine their own salary. It may be worth considering putting in place an employment contract or director's appointment letter, setting out salary terms before gifting any shares or alternatively, giving shareholders the power to approve director's fees or salaries.

Chapter 11

Taxation

11.1 Most FICs will be UK resident for tax purposes (as they will be registered and/or controlled from the UK) and they will be subject to the same corporation tax rules that apply to any other UK company. By their nature, FICs will be carrying on an investment rather than a trading business.

11.2 By their nature FICs are likely to be within the definition of a close company as they will be under the control of five or fewer participators (broadly shareholders) or under the control of their directors. This is especially so given the rights of close family members, spouses, civil partners and trustees of family trusts are all taken into account. Being a close company means FICs will be subject to additional tax rules, such as the transaction in securities legislation and rules on benefits to participators.

11.3 Companies resident in the UK or those that carry on a trade in the UK through a permanent establishment pay corporation tax on their profits which is made up of their income and chargeable gains. Broadly, companies resident in the UK pay corporation tax on their worldwide profits and non-resident companies pay tax on the profits arising in the UK.

11.4 The current main rate of corporation tax is 25% and this applies to all profits for a company that is a close investment holding company ('CIHC'), a non-resident company or for all other companies where profits are over £250,000. For non CIHCs, if profits are £50,000 or less the rate of corporation tax is 19% and for profits between £50,000 and £250,000 marginal rate relief will apply, which means their rate of tax is between 19% and 25% depending on their profits.

11.5 A CIHC is a close company that does not exist for a permitted purpose. A permitted purpose is:

- Trading on a commercial basis;
- Holding rental properties; or
- Holding shares in or making loans to other companies that are under the control or are under common control.

A property owning FIC is likely not to be a CIHC but a FIC investing in equities, will be.

11.6 Profits are calculated by reference to a company's accounting period.

11.7 The profits on income are calculated separately depending on the source of income. The main sources being:

- Trading income.
- Property income.
- Non-trading loan relationships.
- Profits from derivative contracts.
- Non-trading intangible assets income.
- Intellectual property.
- Miscellaneous income.

11.8 Chargeable gains are calculated using the capital gains tax rules but are subject to corporation tax and not capital gains tax. The amount of chargeable gain added to a company's profits, is the total of chargeable gains less allowable losses in that period and allowable losses brought forward from any previous period. Allowable losses cannot normally be offset against trading profits or other income, however trading losses can be offset against chargeable gains.

11.9 Indexation allowance for companies was stopped in December 2017 but can still be claimed up to December 2017.

11.10 When investing for a FIC, care must be taken to understand the nature of the investment and its tax treatment. Some investments, such as corporate bonds, may be within the scope of the loan relationship rules or the rules relating to derivative contracts and in such cases specialist corporate tax advice may be needed. The accounting policies adopted by the FIC will also impact on the tax treatment of such investments.

11.11 Given FICs carry on an investment business they are able to deduct expenses of management. This will usefully include a deduction for the fees of a discretionary fund manager engaged to manage a FICs investment portfolio, or similar charges for advisory or execution only portfolios. Expenses of a capital nature, such as SDLT on a property purchase, will not be deductible but may be taken into account when calculating chargeable gains.

11.12 For accounting purposes it may be necessary to account for some forms of investments (eg investment properties) on a fair value basis, which means the growth or loss on an investment during the accounting period will have to be recognised in the accounts. Deferred tax provisions will take account of the potential tax charges. For tax purposes adjustments may be needed to the accounting profit, as corporation tax on a gain or loss will normally only arise when the asset is actually disposed of (such as an investment property).

Chapter 12

Dividends – General

12.1 A company distributes its post-tax profits to its shareholders by declaring and paying a dividend. Dividends are determined by reference to an accounting period and will either be interim (generally paid during the accounting period) or final (paid after the end of the accounting period). Final dividends are typically approved by shareholders at an AGM and based on a recommendation from the board. Directors are free to declare interim dividends at any time and do not need shareholder approval. Many privately owned companies just pay interim dividends and such dividends only become taxable when paid. When a final dividend has been approved by shareholders, it becomes a debt owed to the shareholders and it becomes taxable at that point. The *Companies Act 2006* does not specify who should declare a dividend so the articles of association for a FIC would typically only give directors the power to declare a dividend so directors can declare both interim and final dividends without shareholder approval.

12.2 UK company law requires a company to have sufficient distributable profits to declare a dividend. A company's profits available for distribution are its 'accumulated, realised profits, so far as not previously utilised by distribution or capitalisation, less its accumulated, realised losses, so far as not previously written off in a reduction or reorganisation of capital duly made' (*Companies Act 2006, s 830(2)*).

12.3 To determine the distributable profits available it is necessary to refer to the company's most recent annual accounts. If these show insufficient distributable profits, it is possible to prepare interim accounts to calculate the figure. The accounting treatment of the company will impact on the distributable reserves available.

12.4 Dividends are paid out of post-tax profits, so no corporation tax deduction is available (*Corporation Tax Act 2009, s 1305*).

12.5 In most cases there will be no withholding tax on the payment of a dividend by a UK company. Exceptions apply to some dividends from types of investment funds. Dividends paid by overseas companies may have withholding tax applied to them. If the UK has a double tax treaty with the country where the paying company is located, withholding tax is reduced or removed entirely.

12.6 Dividends received by a UK company are generally not subject to corporation tax as a result of widely drawn exemptions. Corporation tax is payable if the distribution falls into certain anti-avoidance rules.

12.7 The exemptions for dividends depends on whether the company is regarded as 'small' or not. A small company is one that has 50 or less employees and whose annual turnover and/or annual balance sheet total does not exceed EUR10 million[1] (and provided it is not an OEIC, an authorised unit trust, an insurance company or a friendly society).

12.8 Where the company is small, a dividend is basically exempt if the payer is resident in the UK or in a 'qualifying territory'. A qualifying territory is broadly any country with which the UK has a double tax treaty that includes a non-discrimination clause. The exemption does not apply if the dividend is paid as part of a tax advantaged scheme.

12.9 A dividend paid by a company that is not small is exempt broadly if it falls within certain classes of dividend, including dividends paid in respect of non-redeemable shares, dividends paid to a company that controls the company and dividends paid to a company that owns less than 10% of the shares in the paying company. The exemptions will not apply if the dividend is paid as part of a tax avoidance arrangement.

[1] See *Corporation Tax Act 2009, s 931S* and the Annex to Commission Recommendation 2003/361/EC of 6 May 2003.

Chapter 13

Dividends – Shareholder Position

13.1 The rules on the taxation of dividends for UK resident individuals changed significantly from 6 April 2016. Since then, taxpayers no longer have a deemed tax credit although they do have a dividend allowance (£500 from 6 April 2024). Dividends received up to the allowance are not subject to tax but above the allowance income tax is paid at the following rates:

Basic rate taxpayer	8.75%
Higher rate taxpayer	33.75%
Additional rate taxpayer and trust	39.35%

13.2 One of the disadvantages of using a company to invest personal wealth, is the impact of the two layers of tax paid (ie the tax paid by the company and the tax paid by a shareholder on a distribution).Following the changes in 2016, the impact of this double tax has increased materially The following table illustrates the cost of income being taxed twice:

13.3

	Basic rate Taxpayer	**40% Taxpayer**	**45% Taxpayer & Trusts**
Non dividend income of the FIC	£100	£100	£100
Less corporation tax at 25%	(£25)	(£25)	(£25)
Net income paid as a dividend	£75	£75	£75
Tax at appropriate rate for dividends (8.75%/33.75%/39.35%)	£6.56	£25.31	£29.51
Net balance (Dividend less Tax payable)	£68.44	£49.69	£45.49
Effective tax rate on original £100 of income	**31.56%**	**50.31%**	**54.51%**

13.4 The impact of the double layer of tax, means that a taxpayer will pay a material additional amount of tax on the income that has been received first in the FIC and then subsequently paid to the shareholder as a dividend. At first sight, this suggests FICs are not very attractive, particularly if all available income is to be distributed annually. But, if income is to be accumulated, then the benefits of the lower corporation tax rate will start to reduce the impact of the additional tax paid by shareholders when the profits are distributed.

13.5 The impact of the double tax charge can also be mitigated by:

- investing for dividend income to avoid the initial corporation tax charge, or
- limiting dividends to maximise the dividend allowance and/or personal allowances of shareholders, or
- funding a FIC with debt and taking interest instead of a dividend

Chapter 14

Dividends – Anti-avoidance Legislation

14.1 There are two anti-avoidance provisions to consider in the context of dividends. The first, is the reservation of benefit rules and the second is the settlements legislation.

RESERVATION OF BENEFIT

14.2 As noted in Chapter 8, the reservation of benefit rules were introduced to prevent individuals from receiving a benefit from assets they have given away. If founders of a FIC have retained some shares in the FIC and gifted other shares of a different class to family members, then care is needed to ensure that they are not able to obtain a benefit from the gifted shares.

14.3 A concern arises where founders are the directors of the FIC and have total discretion to determine the level of dividend payable to each shareholder. If such power is used to pay themselves an inflated dividend there is concern that this could be argued to amount to a retained benefit. For example, if parents retained a 10% shareholding and their children had 90% of the shares (shares of a different class but having equal rights to income) and parents used their powers to pay themselves 50% of the profits available for distribution, they will have taken 40% more than they are naturally entitled to, which is arguably a benefit they have retained over the shares given away.

14.4 Where reservation of benefit is a concern, it would be possible through the articles of association or shareholders' agreement, to limit the founders' discretion to pay themselves a dividend that exceeds the natural entitlement of their shares.

SETTLEMENTS LEGISLATION

14.5 The settlements legislation is also relevant to the payment of dividends to shareholders and awareness of the rules is important to avoid unexpected tax charges. The legislation is found in the *Income Tax (Trading and Other Income) Act 2005* ('*ITTOIA 2005*'), *Pt 5, Ch 5* and 'is intended to prevent an individual from gaining a tax advantage by making arrangements which divert his or her income to another person who is liable at a lower rate of tax or is not liable to income tax. It applies only where the settlor has retained an interest in the settled property or income'.[1]

14.6 The legislation applies to trusts, companies, individuals and partnerships. It covers:

- settlor interested trusts;
- settlements for minor children;
- capital sums paid to settlors by a settlement, and
- capital sums paid by a company connected with a settlement.

14.7 HMRC guidance to the settlements legislation can be found in the Trusts, Settlements and Estates Manual at paragraph 4001 onwards. It is a useful summary of the rules although obviously reflecting HMRC's interpretation of the legislation.

14.8 When considering what a settlement is, the definition is so wide that it is actually hard to imagine what could not be caught. It includes any arrangement, trust, disposition or transfer of assets including a series of transactions. There is however an important limitation to the definition, which is that in all cases there must be an element of bounty (*CIR v Plummer* [1979] STC 793). The word bounty suggests something more than just a gift. For example, it has been taken to include an expectation of the settlor's subsequent behaviour.[2]

14.9 In light of the requirement for bounty, a simple way to avoid the application of the Settlements Legislation is to make the arrangement on commercial terms where there is no element bounty.

14.10 Where there is a settlement, it is important to identify who the person is that has provided the funds for the settlement given such person will be regarded as the settlor. The settlor can provide funds either directly or indirectly, and with companies it can sometimes not be immediately obvious who the settlor is. For example:

> Thomas is the sole director and owns all the shares in Propco Ltd, a property investment company. Thomas's father, Freddie, sets up a family trust with £100 and the family trust uses this money to subscribe for new shares at par in Propco Ltd. The trust has been established for the benefit of Thomas's children. Shortly after the issue of the new shares, a dividend is declared and the Trust receives £50,000.

[1] HMRC Manual – Trusts Settlements and Estates Manual paragraph 4015.

[2] See TSEM4105, where HMRC give the example that in *Jones v Garnett* (78 TC 597); [2007] 4 All ER 857 the arrangement was the simple issue of a share in a company and the 'bounty' was provided by the expectation of the settlor's subsequent behaviour.

In this situation, Thomas controlled the arrangement for the issue of the shares at par followed by the payment of the dividend. Thomas is therefore regarded as the true settlor of the settlement from which income of £50,000 arose. The original settlement of £100 by Freddie will probably be disregarded on de-minimis grounds.

14.11 Having established that you have a settlement, and who the settlor is, you then have to consider if the settlor has retained an interest in the settlement. A settlor is deemed to have retained an interest in a settlement if any property or any related property in the settlement is paid, or will or may become payable to, or applicable for, the benefit of the settlor or his spouse or civil partner in any circumstances whatsoever.

14.12 The definition is wide enough that a benefit can still arise to the settlor or their spouse, even if income is paid to a third party, provided there is a benefit to the settlor.

14.13 Where a settlor has retained an interest in a settlement, the income of the settlement will be taxed on the settlor (subject to a few exceptions for certain types of income).

14.14 Given the breadth of these provisions, all gifts between spouses or civil partners would be caught if it wasn't for the important exception to these rules for outright gifts to a spouse or civil partner[3] provided:

- the gift carries a right to the whole of the income, and
- the property given is not wholly or substantially a right to income.

A further condition for the exception is that the outright gift cannot be subject to conditions or arrangements whereby the giver can receive the asset back or receive a benefit from it.

14.15 In the High Court case of *Young v Pearce; Young v Scrutton* (1996) STC 743 the two owners of a profitable company decided to reorganise the share capital of the company by issuing preference shares to their wives. The preference shares had no rights to capital on a winding up and no voting rights. Dividends were paid on the preference shares to the wives who paid tax at lower rates than their husbands. HMRC were able to successfully argue the application of the settlements legislation to tax the dividends on the husbands. The exception did not assist as the preference shares amounted to substantially a right to income due to their limited rights.

14.16 The *Pearce* case can be contrasted with the case of *Jones v Garnett* [2007] STC 1536. In this case, the husband and wife each owned one share in Arctic Systems Ltd. The husband

[3] *ITTOIA, s 626.*

was the sole director and earned all the profits of the company as an IT consultant but taking only a small salary. His wife dealt with book-keeping and administrative work and also received a small salary. Dividends were paid equally to the husband and wife but the level of dividend was substantially greater than it would have been had the husband drawn a salary commensurate with his earning power. HMRC sought to tax the husband on part of the dividends paid to his wife under the Settlements Legislation. The case ended in the House of Lords where it was held that the arrangements did amount to a settlement but the exclusion for outright gifts to spouses applied, so that HMRC lost the case.

14.17 These two cases highlight the importance of the rights attaching to the shares and the potential impact on their tax treatment. In *Jones v Garnett*, the wife's shares had rights to income and capital so could not be treated as simply a right to income, whereas in the *Pearce* case, the wife's shares only had a right to income.

14.18 To provide flexibility on the payment of dividends to different shareholders, it is common to create different share classes, as in the *Pearce* case above. This enables the directors to declare different rates of dividend to each share class or to pay dividends at different times. Often referred to as having 'alphabet shares', a company may create lots of different share classes giving each different class of share a different letter of the alphabet. An alternative approach is for a shareholder to waive their entitlement to a dividend. Dividend waivers are normally documented in a deed to ensure enforceability and avoid the need for consideration. The effect is the same as alphabet shares but given it requires the shareholder to take action, it is not the preferred choice of FICs where control is preferred to be with the directors. Paying dividends under these arrangements can be caught by the settlements legislation.

14.19 For example, Albert sets up a FIC and owns A shares and his wife Rachel owns B shares. The A and B shares rank equally for income. The FIC generates profits of £50,000 and Albert decides to declare a dividend of £35,000 on the B shares. By not declaring a dividend on the A shares Albert has entered into a bounteous arrangement as there are insufficient profits to pay the same level of dividend to the A shares. The settlement arises from the arrangement and as no asset has been transferred, the exception for outright gifts to spouses does not apply. As a result, HMRC may seek to apply *ITTOIA, s 624* and attribute the excess over a 50% share of the profits, ie £10,000 of the dividend paid to Rachel as Albert's income.

14.20 In another example, Hilary owns 75 shares in her company Hill Ltd and her husband Frank owns the other 25 shares. The company makes a profit of £50,000. Hilary waives her right to any dividend and then the company declares a dividend of £1,400 per share, and Frank, who had no other income, receives a dividend of £35,000. The act of waiving the right to any dividend and then declaring the dividend to Frank can be seen as a settlement. The required element of bounty is present because there are insufficient profits to pay a dividend at the same rate on the remaining 75 shares. Again, the settlement arises from the arrangements, as no property has been transferred and the exception for outright gifts to spouses does not apply. The settlement is one of income and as such the settlements legislation may be applied in these circumstances with the result that £22,500 of the dividend paid to Frank is attributed to Hilary under *ITTOIA, s 624*.

14.21 It is worth noting that *ITTOIA, s 624* is only relevant where the settlor or their spouse has received a benefit. At first sight, it may be seen that using alphabet shares to pay disproportionate dividends to adult children may not be caught. But, it is clear that a wide interpretation is given to the phrase 'receiving a benefit' and therefore consideration should be given as to whether a parent has received a benefit when a disproportionate dividend is paid to their adult children.

14.22 Using alphabet shares in a FIC structure is common as the risk of the application of the settlements legislation only arises when disproportionate dividends are paid on the alphabet shares. If a policy is taken to only pay dividends that are proportionate to the entitlement of each class of shares to the profits, then the key element of bounty will not be present and there should be no risk. This can either be done by simply applying the principal when declaring dividends or by writing these rules into the articles or shareholders' agreement of the company as mentioned earlier.

14.23 In addition to the above, *ITTOIA, s 629* also taxes income received by minor children where it derives from property gifted to them by their parents either directly or indirectly.

14.24 For example, Barry and Sue each own 50 of the 100 issued ordinary shares in their FIC. They each decide to give 10 shares to each of their children aged 8 and 12. The children each then hold 20 shares, 10 from each parent. Any dividends paid to the children whilst they remain minors will be treated as the income of Barry and Sue under the settlements legislation.

14.25 As before care needs to be taken over arrangements whereby the parents are seen as indirectly providing the assets. For example, Bill has a property company and allows his mother in law Wendy to subscribe for 30% of the shares at par. Shortly after subscribing for the shares, Wendy gifts the shares to Bill's two children. In this situation Bill will be seen as the settlor of those shares as he was behind the arrangement which allowed Wendy to subscribe for the shares at par. Dividends paid to his children whilst they are minors will be taxed on him.

14.26 A gift of shares by a parent to a discretionary trust of which a minor child is a beneficiary will also be caught by these rules when income is distributed to the minor child.

Chapter 15

Funding a FIC

SHARE SUBSCRIPTIONS

15.1 Cash funds are usually introduced into a company either by subscribing for shares or by way of a loan.

15.2 All companies limited by shares will be required to issue at least one share on incorporation. Each share has a par value, typically £1 and the shares issued on incorporation are always acquired at their par value. After incorporation, shares can be issued at a premium, for example each share may have a nominal value of £0.10 but each subscriber agrees to pay £1, £0.90 will then represent the share premium for each share.

15.3 No tax issues arise on subscription for shares at par value or at a premium on incorporation or shortly thereafter (assuming the company has not acquired any other assets in the meantime).

15.4 The price paid on subscription of the shares will form the base cost of the shares. The *Taxation of Chargeable Gains Act 1992 (TCGA 1992), s 17* does not apply to deem a market value as on the acquisition of the shares by way of subscription there is no corresponding disposal by the company.[1]

15.5 A company is often incorporated with a single subscriber share and then additional shares are issued subsequently. This has some practical benefits, namely:

- Companies House do not like 'joint subscribers' so issuing shares in the name of two or more individuals who are acting as trustees is difficult;
- subscribers may have to sign the incorporation forms (online filing is not possible for an unlimited company) and obtaining lots of signatures may be difficult, and

[1] *TCGA 1992, s 17(2).*

- a company has to be formed to open a bank or investment account and shares cannot be paid for until the company has a means to hold the funds. It is therefore easier to issue most shares at a time when they can be paid for straightaway.

15.6 Where parents or grandparents establish a FIC for their family, they can either subscribe for the shares and then gift them to children/grandchildren or they can enter into arrangements whereby the children/grandchildren subscribe for the shares directly with the FIC but on the understanding that the parent/grandparents will pay the subscription price.

15.7 If shares are to be gifted, such gift will be deemed to have occurred at market value and accordingly there is potential for either a capital gain or a capital loss to arise for the donor, depending on the number of shares gifted and the rights attaching to the shares. The base cost for the donee will also be the market value of the shares. For this reason, it is often easier for the family members to subscribe directly for shares.

15.8 The acquisition of shares can give rise to concerns under the employment related securities regime found in *ITEPA 2003, Pt 7* especially where a family member is or will become a director or employee. The definition of what is an employment related security is broad and includes deeming provisions which on the face of it can be a concern. If the shares in a FIC were caught, it is also likely that any shares issued in a FIC would be subject to a number of restrictions which will mean that they would fall within the definition of restricted securities. Thankfully there is an important exception which provides relief from these concerns, for rights or opportunities to acquire shares made available by an individual in the normal course of the 'domestic, family or personal relationships' of that person (*ITEPA 2003, s 431B(a), (b)*). In the normal course of establishing most FIC, its main purpose is to facilitate estate planning for the family. There is no commercial relationship between the family members in this case. This exception also applies to the founders of the FIC, who receive shares as a result of their own personal planning.

15.9 Additional shares can always be issued by a FIC at any time it wishes, but to avoid tax charges arising from value shifting, it is always important to pay market value for the new shares. Appropriate share valuation advice is therefore needed to determine the right price to pay for the shares. To the extent the price is above the nominal value, the excess will be regarded as share premium.

Gifts to a Company

15.10 A gift to a company is treated as a chargeable lifetime transfer as it cannot be a potentially exempt transfer under the *Inheritance Tax Act 1984* (*IHTA 1984), s 3A* as such gifts have to be made to an individual (or certain trusts). Accordingly, a gift to a company will trigger a 20% lifetime charge on the value of the gift (which is strictly the loss to the estate) subject to any applicable exemptions.

15.11 If the gift is made to a company that is owned entirely by the donor, there is an argument that there is no reduction in the value of the donor's estate and therefore the value of the gift is nil, resulting in no actual inheritance tax liability. This may appear to offer the opportunity to gift assets to a FIC, but any gift will increase the value of the shares, so a subsequent gift of those shares is likely to result in gain, triggering a potential capital gains tax charge.

Sale of Assets

15.12 Where cash is not available, assets can be sold to a FIC either in return for an IOU or an issue of shares.

15.13 For example, Andy has a commercial property worth £1.5 million which he wants to give to his children but he wants to retain control over the property, ensuring that it is properly managed and so he can accumulate the rental income to fund other investments. Andy can first establish a FIC with a nominal share capital and then agree to sell the property at its market value to the FIC. This will trigger a disposal for capital gains tax purposes and the company will be liable for Stamp Duty Land Tax. The consideration can be left outstanding as a debt (interest free and repayable on demand). Andy may then assign the debt in parts of £500,000 to his three children, Jack, Mary and Lily. The assignments will be potentially exempt transfers by Andy, so as long as he survives seven years from the date of the gift, no inheritance tax will arise. The children can then subscribe £500,000 for shares and agree to set off their debt in payment of the subscription price.

The resulting structure will be:

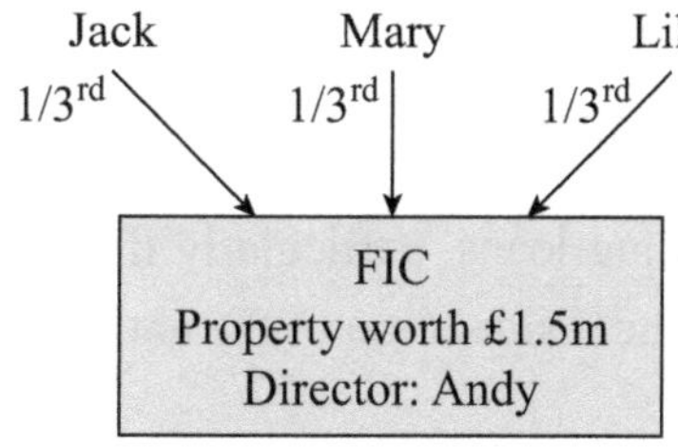

Shareholder	Percentage interest	Subscription price paid
Jack	One third	£500,000
Mary	One third	£500,000
Lily	One third	£500,000
Total		£1,500,000

Share for Share Exchanges

15.14 Once a FIC is established, it may enter into arrangements to acquire shares in another company for an issue of shares in itself and provided the exchange falls into the rules for reorganisations under *TCGA 1992, ss 126–136*, there will be no disposal of shares.

15.15 *TCGA 1992, s 135* deals with the exchange of securities for those in another company and provides that the reorganisation rules will apply where the company that issues shares in consequence of an exchange holds or in consequence of the exchange will hold more than 25% of the ordinary share capital of the target. The reorganisation rules are subject to anti-avoidance provisions, in particular *TCGA 1992, s 137* which states that there must be a genuine commercial reason for the exchange of shares.

15.16 For example, Arthur's parents left in their Will 25% of the shares in the family trading company, worth £500,000, to a discretionary settlement. Arthur has separately established a FIC the shares in which are owned by his children. The FIC currently has £1 million of equity investments. The trustees of the family trust decide that it would be preferable for them to diversify their investments and recognise that they could do so if they invested through the FIC rather than hold the trading company shares. The trustees therefore agree with the FIC to 'sell' the trading company shares in return for an issue of shares. Given the respective values of the companies the FIC will issue sufficient shares to the trustees so that they are left holding a 33% interest in the enlarged FIC. The FIC is now worth £1.5 million, but the trustees' interest worth £500,000 is now much more diversified than it was prior to the transaction.

Using Loans

15.17 Loans are an attractive way to fund a FIC because they:

- are flexible, especially when repayable on demand, and
- provide an easy way to return capital.

However, before deciding on making loans, particularly if loans are the preferred basis for the majority of a FICs funding, careful consideration of the anti-avoidance rules is needed.

15.18 Loans made to a FIC on commercial terms should not cause any tax issues, other than the obvious tax charge for the recipient of the interest. Such loans should be outside the settlements legislation as there is no element of bounty and should avoid a challenge under the transaction in securities rules as the interest charge is evidence that the arrangements have not been entered into for the purpose of gaining an income tax advantage.

15.19 A loan made on interest free, repayable on demand terms, should not give rise to a transfer of value for inheritance tax purposes as the value of the loan is equal to the amount of it.[2] However, if the loan is not repayable for a fixed period, the value of the loan will be reduced and a chargeable transfer may arise. For this reason, most loans will be at least repayable on demand.

15.20 The two main areas of concern for interest free or discounted loans are the transaction in securities rules and the settlements legislation.

Transactions in Securities (TiS)

15.21 Under the *Income Tax Act 2007 (ITA 2007), ss 682–713*, HMRC has the power to counteract tax advantages obtained in consequence of one or more transactions in securities where an income tax advantage was the purpose of the arrangements. The rules only apply to close companies and the onus rests on HMRC to prove the TiS regime applies.

15.22 The TiS regime applies where a person is a party to one or more 'transactions in securities' and a person (not necessarily the same person) obtains an income tax advantage in consequence of the transactions. Either Condition A or Condition B has to be met and the main purpose or one of the main purposes of the person being involved in the transactions in securities was to obtain the income tax advantage.

15.23 The definition of a transaction in securities in *ITA 2007, s 684(2)* is wide and includes subscribing for shares, altering share rights or returning share capital.

15.24 Condition A is the most likely condition to be in point and it is set out at *ITA 2007, s 685(2)* as follows:

> 'Condition A is that, as a result of the transaction in securities or any one or more of the transactions in securities, a relevant person receives relevant consideration in connection with—
>
> (a) the distribution, transfer or realisation of assets of a close company,
> (b) the application of assets of a close company in discharge of liabilities, or
> (c) the direct or indirect transfer of assets of one close company to another close company,
>
> and the relevant person does not pay or bear income tax on the consideration.'

15.25 The issue to consider is whether or not the repayment by the company of an interest free loan is capable of being caught under the TiS regime.

[2] See Inheritance Tax Manual 14317.

15.26 The first question is: has a person been a party to a transaction in securities. A simple loan is not a security, so it is hard to see how making a loan would be regarded as a transaction in securities, however a subscription for shares will be a transaction in securities. The income tax advantage being obtained does not have to come directly from the transaction in securities, it just has to be part of an overall arrangement. Accordingly, in order to come within the regime there must be a link between a subscription for shares and the loan. The strength of connection does not have to be strong but it does need to be shown as part of the same overall arrangement. This may be difficult to prove.

15.27 The second condition is that 'relevant consideration' has to be received. Relevant consideration is defined as profits that would otherwise be available to pay a dividend. It is likely that a repayment of a loan is funded out of profits of the company, so it is likely that 'relevant consideration' is being received.

15.28 The next condition is that the person has obtained an income tax advantage. Given the funds are being received in the form of a loan repayment, no income tax would normally be payable, so it is arguable that a form of income tax advantage has been obtained.

15.29 Finally, was the obtaining of the income tax advantage the main purpose of the arrangements? This will obviously come down to the facts of the case, but it is not impossible to see an argument for this. For example, Peter sets up a company subscribing £100 for 100 ordinary shares, he then lends £5 million to the company and invests in equities that pay dividends. The dividends create profits in the company, but Peter chooses to use those profits to repay his loan, rather than pay a dividend. In this situation it is possible to see that there is a connection between the initial share subscription and the loan. The loan repayments are received tax free but are being funded out of profits which are 'relevant consideration' for the purposes of the legislation. It is likely that Peter's motive for arranging his investments in this way was to obtain an income tax advantage. He has invested his money but is able to receive regular returns on his investment which are not subject to income tax. The dividends received by the company are not subject to tax (for the reasons outlined above) which only makes the arrangements more attractive. It is noted of course that the advantage is only a deferral, as income tax will ultimately be payable on the profits generated, once the original loan is repaid (and assuming the company is not wound up although that itself may trigger income tax charges under the TiS regime). Overall the arrangement is not that dissimilar from the tax effects of an investment bond, which of course is something that has been accepted for some time.

15.30 There is an argument that funding a close company by way of a loan is very common and by virtue of how common it is, it arguably makes the arrangement more commercial when compared with other arrangements such as issuing redeemable preference shares.

15.31 The application of the TiS provisions to most loans made to established companies is very unlikely as there will be no link to a transaction in securities.

Settlements Legislation

15.32 The structure of the Settlements Legislation found in the *Income Tax (Trading and Other Income) Act 2005* (*ITTOIA 2005*), *Pt 5, Ch 5* is discussed above in the context of dividends and as noted the definition of a settlement is very wide and can catch any arrangement, trust, disposition or transfer of assets. Such a wide definition will include an agreement to lend money to a FIC. However, as also noted, for a settlement to exist there must be an element of bounty. The existence of bounty was something considered in *IRC v Levy* [1982] STC 442.

15.33 In the *Levy* case, Mr Levy owned 99% of the shares in a company that dealt in stocks and shares. Mr Levy and his wife made several interest free, repayable on demand loans to the company. HMRC argued that the interest free loans represented bounty and that a settlement existed with the result that the income generated by the company on the capital lent to it, should be taxed on Mr Levy. It was held that the test for determining bounty was subjective not objective and the transactions should be looked at as a whole. Mr Levy gave up something, but in circumstances where he anticipated and intended to secure from those transactions a compensating advantage to himself (as majority shareholder). There was found to be no bounty and therefore no settlement. This case is helpful when looking at structuring personal investment companies.

15.34 Whilst the *Levy* case is helpful, it does raise the question, what if Mr Levy had not been the major shareholder? For example, say Mr Levy had made interest free loans to a company where his minor children were the major shareholders. In that situation Mr Levy would still have given up something but the benefit would be received by his minor children who are the shareholders. Looking at the situation in the round, there may well be an argument that the required element of bounty exists in that situation so that there is a settlement.

15.35 If a settlement exists, the next question to consider is, has the settlor retained an interest in the settled property. In this case, Mr Levy was the settlor as he has provided the relevant funds. HMRC may argue that he has retained an interest in the loaned funds because he has only lent the funds. But an alternative argument is that Mr Levy has merely exchanged the money lent for the right to have the money repaid (a 'chose in action'). Whilst he has clearly retained an interest in the chose in action, this asset does not give rise to any income on which Mr Levy may be taxed. Mr Levy has no legal interest or right to the income generated by the company from the funds he has lent to it, therefore he cannot be taxed on that income.

15.36 Another technical defence to the settlements legislation in respect of interest free loans is found in the *Corporation Tax Act 2009 (CTA 2009), s 3(1)* which precludes the application of the Income Taxes Acts applying to a UK company subject to corporation tax. Perhaps, unhelpfully, *CTA 2009, s 3(2)* goes on to say that *s 3(1)* does not apply where a company is 'acting in a fiduciary or representative capacity'. If a loan is a settlement, it may be suggested that the company is holding the trust fund as a fiduciary so *CTA 2009, s 3(1)* wouldn't help. Although the potential role as a fiduciary only exists if you apply the income tax rules first.

15.37 In order to avoid a potential challenge under the settlements legislation the solution is to charge interest at a commercial rate. Charging a commercial rate of interest removes any argument that there is bounty in the arrangements.

Chapter 16

Other Tax Issues

CLOSE COMPANY RULES

16.1 A FIC is very likely to be regarded as a close company and it will therefore be subject to the special tax rules and anti-avoidance provisions that apply to such companies. A close company is broadly one that is controlled by five or fewer participators. For this purpose, the rights of associates are included, and the definition of an associate includes a spouse, civil partner, parent, child or remoter issue, siblings, or trustees of family trusts. A participator includes anyone that holds or has a right to acquire share capital or voting rights in a company or a loan creditor.

16.2 Close company rules, include provisions which will tax loans made by the company to shareholders (either directly or indirectly), including trustees of a trust, where such loans are outstanding at the end of an accounting period, unless repaid within nine months from the end of the accounting period. From 6 April 2016, the tax charge is at the higher rate applicable to dividends, 32.5%. When loans are repaid, the tax paid by the company can be reclaimed, so the effect of the rules is more a cash flow issue for the company.

16.3 There are special rules that apply to benefits provided to participators and their associates, which results in such benefits being taxed as a distribution. The effect of these rules is that expenditure incurred by a close company in providing living or other accommodation, entertainment, domestic or other services or other benefits or facilities of any kind for any participator or the associate of any participator, is treated as a distribution and taxed accordingly. It is worth noting that the company that provides such benefits cannot get any tax deduction for their cost, when treated as a distribution. There is an exemption from these provisions where such benefits are provided to employees or their family and are taxed under the benefit in kind rules.

16.4 There are also specific rules for transfers of assets by a close company which are not made on arm's length terms and inheritance tax rules which deem gifts made by the company to be made by the shareholders in certain circumstances. Shareholders may also be deemed to have made chargeable lifetime transfers where certain changes are made to the company's share capital.

16.5 Careful consideration of the close company rules is necessary when dealing with any reorganisation, unusual distribution or provision of assets or benefits to shareholders or loan creditors in a FIC.

GAAR and DOTAS

16.6 When undertaking any planning it is necessary to bear in mind both the general anti-abuse rule ('GAAR') and the requirements of the disclosure of tax avoidance schemes regime ('DOTAS'). The rules are by necessity complex and what follows is just a brief comment in the context of forming a straightforward FIC.

16.7 In respect of GAAR, it is hard to see how forming a company can be regarded as unacceptable tax avoidance. There is nothing contrived or abnormal about incorporating a company, giving shares to family members and operating an investment business. Growing wealth in a FIC which is subject to corporation tax, even if benefiting from the relief applicable to dividends, is not exploiting shortcomings in the legislation, it is merely applying the rules. It also should not be forgotten that additional tax is payable when the profits are distributed to shareholders, so any benefit is only really in the accumulation of the profits within the FIC. It will however come down to the facts of the arrangements proposed in any particular case as to whether or not GAAR is a matter of concern.

16.8 The scope of DOTAS for inheritance tax was extended from 1 April 2018 by *The Inheritance Tax Avoidance Schemes (Prescribed Description of Arrangements) Regulations 2017* which provides as follows:

> 'Arrangements fall within the description in this regulation if it would be reasonable to expect an informed observer (having studied the arrangements and having regard to all relevant circumstances) to conclude that condition 1 and condition 2 are met.
>
> Condition 1 is that the main purpose, or one of the main purposes, of the arrangements is to enable a person to obtain one or more of the following advantages in relation to inheritance tax (the "tax advantage")—
>
> (a) the avoidance or reduction of a relevant property entry charge;
>
> (b) the avoidance or reduction of a charge to inheritance tax under section 64, 65, 72 or 94 of IHTA 1984;
>
> (c) the avoidance or reduction of a charge to inheritance tax arising from the application of section 102, 102ZA, 102A or 102B of the Finance Act 1986 in circumstances where there is also no charge to income tax under Schedule 15 to the Finance Act 2004 (charge to income tax on benefits received by former owner of property);

(d) a reduction in the value of a person's estate without giving rise to a chargeable transfer or potentially exempt transfer.

Condition 2 is that the arrangements involve one or more contrived or abnormal steps without which the tax advantage could not be obtained.'

16.9 When forming a FIC, shares are either given to family members or shares are issued to family members but paid for on their behalf, generally by parents or grandparents. In either case, this is a gift so there is a reduction in the value of a person's estate but there is no doubt that the gift will give rise to a potentially exempt transfer. On this basis, Condition 1 is not met so forming a typical FIC would not be within the scope of DOTAS.

16.10 Whilst one of the main purposes of establishing a FIC may be inheritance tax planning, it should not be forgotten that the arrangement may be disclosable under the DOTAS regime for other taxes, being capital gains tax, income tax, corporation tax, stamp duty land tax and annual tax on enveloped dwellings. Consideration of the relevant provisions would be required depending on the facts of each case.

Chapter 17

Accounting Issues

17.1 Family Investment Companies (FICs) are a tax planning vehicle for individuals that wish to pass on wealth (eg, to children or other family members). The structure of a FIC is usually a limited company, but it can also be unlimited. The main advantage of structuring the FIC as an unlimited entity is that there is increased privacy for shareholders given that there are no filing requirements at Companies House for unlimited FICs. FICs that are structured as a limited company must lodge their accounts with Companies House usually within nine months of the FIC's balance sheet date.

The remainder of this chapter assumes that the FIC is an incorporated entity.

As a FIC is usually a private company, incorporated under the Companies Act 2006, it will be required to prepare accounts that give a true and fair view. The accounts of the FIC must comply with the requirements of UK and Ireland Generally Accepted Accounting Practice (GAAP) and the *Companies Act 2006*.

17.2 In the UK and Republic of Ireland, companies are required to prepare their financial statements using:

- FRS 101 *Reduced Disclosure Framework* which sets out the disclosure exemptions for the individual financial statements of a subsidiary (including an intermediate parent) and ultimate parent companies that otherwise apply the recognition, measurement and disclosure requirements of IFRS® Accounting Standards. In practice, it is rare for a FIC to apply FRS 101.
- FRS 102 *The Financial Reporting Standard applicable in the UK and Republic of Ireland* which is the 'main' accounting standard in the UK and Republic of Ireland. FRS 102 includes Section 1A *Small Entities* which provides the presentation and disclosure requirements for companies that are small in the eyes of the Companies Act 2006 (Section 1A is an optional section).
- FRS 105 *The Financial Reporting Standard applicable to the Micro-entities Regime*. This standard can only be applied by eligible micro-entities and offers a significantly reduced

disclosure regime as well as a prescriptive means of preparing accounts. Micro-entities preparing their financial statements in accordance with FRS 105 need not consider any additional disclosure requirements to achieve a true and fair view. The correct application of FRS 105 presumes a true and fair view has been achieved.

FRS 100 Application of Financial Reporting Requirements, FRS 103 *Insurance Contracts* and FRS 104 *Interim Financial Reporting* are beyond the scope of this Chapter.

INVESTMENTS

17.3 For FICs that prepare their accounts under FRS 102 (including the presentation and disclosure requirements of Section 1A), Section 11 *Basic Financial Instruments* or Section 12 *Other Financial Instruments Issues* will apply. Whether an investment falls under the scope of Section 11 or Section 12 will depend on the characteristics of the investment. Basic financial assets will fall under the scope of Section 11; whereas non-basic ones will fall under the scope of Section 12. Most financial assets that fall under the scope of FRS 102, Section 12 are measured at fair value.

On initial recognition, an investment will usually be recognised at cost. Cost is adjusted for transaction costs, except in the initial measurement of financial assets that are subsequently measured at fair value through profit or loss (FRS 102, para 11.13).

Generally, after initial recognition, investments (other than investment properties – see **5.4** below) can be measured using either:

- Cost less impairment; or
- Fair value through profit or loss.

If investments are publicly traded or their fair value can otherwise be measured reliably, the investment is measured at fair value through profit or loss (FRS 102, para 11.14(d)(iv)). All other such investments are measured at cost less impairment. Investments in another group entity that are within the scope of FRS 102, Section 11 can also be measured at fair value through other comprehensive income or profit or loss (FRS 102, para 11.14(d)(ii)).

FRS 105 does not allow the use of fair value or revaluation amounts. All investments will therefore be measured at cost less impairment.

INVESTMENT PROPERTY

17.4 Some FICs include investment property on the balance sheet. Investment properties are dealt with in FRS 102, Section 16 *Investment Property*. Section 16 requires all investment property to be initially recognised at cost, which usually comprises:

- Initial purchase price
- Legal and brokerage fees
- Property transfer taxes
- All other directly incremental costs of acquiring the investment property

After initial recognition at cost, investment property must be remeasured to fair value at each balance sheet date. Fair value gains and losses are recognised in profit or loss (FRS 102, para 16.7). In addition, deferred tax consequences must be brought into account.

It should be emphasised that fair value gains, net of any relevant deferred tax consequences, are **non-distributable profits**. This is because the gain is an unrealised gain for distribution purposes. The FIC may choose to segregate these non-distributable profits in a 'non-distributable reserve' (although there is nothing in company law that requires this). Alternatively, the FIC can choose to accumulate distributable and non-distributable profits in retained earnings (profit and loss reserves).

If the FIC prepares its accounts under FRS 105, it cannot subsequently measure the investment property at fair value. This is because the Fair Value Accounting Rules in company law do not apply to micro-entities. Consequently, the micro-entity must measure the investment property under the cost model (cost less depreciation less impairment).

MANAGEMENT EXPENSES

17.5 Expenses incurred by the FIC in managing its investments will be recognised as such in the profit and loss account (where they do not meet the recognition criteria for recognition on the balance sheet). This includes investment managers' fees and remuneration that is paid to the directors and employees of the FIC. As with 'normal' limited companies, expenses may be incurred by the FIC that are not allowable for tax relief (eg, entertaining expenditure).
It is important that the directors ensure the FIC maintain proper accounting records in the event of any inquiries into the FIC's corporation tax return by HM Revenue and Customs.

DISCLOSURE REQUIREMENTS IN THE FINANCIAL STATEMENTS

17.6 As noted earlier, a FIC that is structured as a limited company is required to prepare accounts in accordance with UK and Ireland GAAP.

Where the FIC prepares its accounts in accordance with FRS 102, including the presentation and disclosure requirements of Section 1A, it must comply with the disclosure requirements in that Section. It should also be emphasised that disclosures **beyond those required by Section 1A** may be required in order to provide a true and fair view. This will, of course, require the use of professional judgement in deciding which additional disclosures to make.

For FICs preparing accounts in accordance with FRS 105, the disclosure requirements are far less detailed. FRS 105, Section 6 *Notes to the Financial Statements* sets out the disclosure requirements as follows:

'(a) off-balance sheet arrangements as required by section 410A of the **Act** (see paragraph 6A.1 of Appendix A to this section);

(b) employee numbers as required by section 411 of the Act (see paragraph 6A.2 of Appendix A to this section);

(c) advances, credit and guarantees granted to directors as required by section 413 of the Act (see paragraph 6A.3 of Appendix A to this section); and

(d) financial commitments, guarantees and contingencies required by regulation 5A of, and paragraph 57 of Part 3 of Schedule 1 to, the **Small Companies Regulations** (see paragraphs 6A.4 and 6A.5 of Appendix A to this section).'[1]

[1] FRS 105, para 6.2 (a) to (d).

Chapter 18

Use of Trusts

18.1 A trust has for generations been the preferred vehicle for estate planning purposes. A trust enables wealth to be moved out of the estates of senior family members with a view to reducing inheritance tax whilst not giving up control of the family wealth, ensuring that it is properly managed and protected for subsequent generations.

18.2 A key advantage is flexibility. For example, a discretionary trust can be established for a wide class of beneficiaries, including the unborn. It can also have a power to add or exclude beneficiaries. The trustees can have complete discretion to determine which individuals may benefit from the trust's income and/or capital. This flexibility is a significant advantage compared to a FIC which can only pay its profits to its shareholders or employees (although it can of course largely employ anyone).

18.3 The disadvantage of a trust is its tax treatment, particularly since 2006 where nearly all new trusts will fall within the relevant property regime. It is now only possible to fund a trust with cash up to the available nil rate band of an individual or with surplus income, if a 20% entry charge is to be avoided. Whilst utilising these reliefs to fund a trust is worthwhile planning, in some cases it is not sufficient, hence the use of FICs. A discretionary trust will also pay income tax and capital gains tax at the highest rates.

18.4 Using a trust in combination with a FIC, helps to mitigate some of the tax disadvantages whilst retaining some of the flexibility. This is achieved by having a family trust as a shareholder in the FIC structure. The shares held by the trust can then be held:

- to benefit as yet unborn family members, as the trustees can hold such shares until grandchildren are born and can either benefit them as beneficiaries or transfer the shares to them at a later time;
- to provide income received from the FIC in the form of dividends, to benefit anyone within the class of beneficiaries which may include individuals who are not direct shareholders, and
- to control the receipt of taxable income in the trust, as the FIC can defer declaring dividends to the trust until the income is needed reducing the trust's liability to tax.

18.5 In addition to the tax advantages, having a trust as one of the shareholders in a FIC has three other material advantages, namely:

1 The trust acts as an additional shareholder, helping to ensure that each family member has a smaller percentage interest in the FIC. This potentially makes the value of the family member's holding worth a little less, especially if it takes the holding below a key threshold, such as from 51% to 49% or 26% to 24%.

2 The trustees of the trust will be able to exercise the voting rights of the shares they hold and whilst they must not exercise those voting rights in a way that is detrimental to their beneficiaries, this may still provide a useful additional level of control.

3 The discretionary trust can provide greater protection for the shares it holds than the shares held directly by a family member, in the event of a claim such as on divorce.

18.6 If a discretionary trust holds shares in a FIC, care needs to be taken if dividends are paid from the FIC to the trust and then distributed to a beneficiary. As noted, discretionary trusts pay income tax at the highest rates, which for dividends is 39.35%. Tax paid by the discretionary trust is then added to a 'tax pool'. If the income of the trust is distributed to a beneficiary it will be treated as trust income and will carry a tax credit of 45%. The amount of the tax credit is deducted from the trust's tax pool, and if the tax pool is insufficient to match the tax credit, the trust has to pay the shortfall. The beneficiary is entitled to the 45% tax credit and if they pay tax at a lower rate, they will be able to reclaim the excess tax.

18.7

Example:

Assume a new discretionary trust receives a dividend from its FIC of £20,000, the tax calculation for the discretionary trust would be as follows (rates as at 2019/20):

		Gross
		£
Total income liable at rate applicable to trusts		20,000
Standard Rate Band		(1,000)
Total Income Taxable at the Trust Rate		19,000
Tax Due		Total
		£
Dividend Rate at 7.5%	£1,000	75
Trust Dividend Rate at 39.35%	**£19,000**	7,476
		7,551

The tax of £7,551 would be added to the tax pool.

After the payment of the tax, the trustees would be left with income of £12,449. If the Trustees decided to pass on the full benefit of this income to the beneficiary, this would result in the following:

Distribution (deemed net)	12,449
Deemed tax credit at 45%	10,185
	22,634
Tax pool	7,551
Less tax credit	10,185
Shortfall payable by Trustees	2,634

As the deemed tax credit is greater than the tax pool, the trustees would have to find a further £2,634in tax. To avoid the payment of further tax, the trustees should limit their distribution to the beneficiary to £9,229, which has a deemed tax credit of £7,551, leaving £3,220 of income in the trust.

18.8 To avoid the complexity described above, if the trustees want a beneficiary to receive the benefit of dividends paid by a FIC to a trust they should consider granting the beneficiary a life interest in all or part of the trust fund. The trustees can then mandate for future dividends to be paid directly to the beneficiary from the FIC, ie not through the trust's bank account. Creating a life interest in this way and then mandating for the income to be paid direct to the beneficiary reduces the trust's tax compliance as they no longer need to report the dividend income. The beneficiary will instead report the dividend income on their personal tax return. It is worth noting that creating a life interest can be done on a revocable basis, so the trustees retain the ability to turn off the income tap if they wish.

BARE TRUSTS

18.9 Bare trusts are appropriate where there are minor children as minors should not hold shares in their own name as they are unable to exercise their voting power or otherwise deal with the shares (such as sell or transfer them).

18.10 A bare trust should be evidenced by a formal legal document that states that the trust fund is held by the trustee(s) absolutely for the benefit of a named beneficiary.

18.11 In the case of a bare trust, the trust fund is the beneficiary's absolute property and, for beneficiaries under the age of 18, legally only their minority prevents them from calling for the trust property to be transferred to them. Strictly the beneficiary is entitled to insist that the trust funds are transferred into their sole name on attaining the age of 18. In practice many children are unlikely to seek to enforce their powers through the courts, giving parents practical control if not legal control.

18.12 It is worth noting that bare trusts do not provide as much asset protection from financial claims as a formal trust structure because the beneficiary is legally absolutely entitled. However, in a divorce situation, it's arguably better than the assets being in the beneficiary's own name as it would give scope for argument that those assets should be held outside the divisible pot as 'inherited wealth'. If considerable funds are built up within bare trust arrangements, the beneficiaries would be well advised to seek other forms of protection in the event of marriage, such as a pre-marital agreement.

Chapter 19

Protection

19.1 A key part of estate planning is to protect wealth for future generations. There are a number of risks to family wealth including poor investment decisions, bankruptcy and of course divorce. A FIC can provide some protection from all of these risks, not least by ensuring that the funds in the FIC are properly managed and invested for the benefit of all shareholders.

19.2 A FIC can't prevent a shareholder becoming bankrupt, but at least the articles can include a mechanism to buy the shares back from the trustee in bankruptcy at an open market value, retaining the shares in the family and keeping the assets of the FIC protected. Similar rules can also apply on divorce.

19.3 When a shareholder divorces, the family court will look to all of the couple's financial resources to determine what an appropriate financial settlement is. The priority of the court is always going to be the needs of the parties. Shares in a FIC are likely to be seen as a resource.

19.4 The principle that a company is a separate legal entity from its shareholders has been firmly upheld in the decision of *Petrodel Resources Ltd v Prest* [2013] UKSC 34; [2013] 3 WLR 1 (SC). Not only that, but if the company has been set up and used for legitimate purposes (eg tax efficiency, passing wealth down the generations, general wealth protection) then the corporate veil will not be pierced.

19.5 However, it will also be necessary to ensure as far as possible that the company controller/shareholder cannot be deemed to have a beneficial interest in the company's assets. The following issues would assist:

- FICs involving multiple shareholders (which is of course the norm) offer an additional layer of protection, because the court would find it harder to assign the whole beneficial interest in any property held by the company to only one of the shareholders, given that it would prejudice the other shareholders.
- Where the assets are being 'introduced' to the company by the family of the company's controller/shareholder, the *Matrimonial Causes Act 1973* ('*MCA 1973*'), *s 24(1)a* cannot

apply because it would be the family, and not the shareholder, who would be 'entitled' to the property. Family investment companies set up in order to protect the following generations from claims on divorce will therefore be protected in this way.

- If the company is a trading company rather than a property holding company, it will be far harder to trace any current assets back to any initial injection of wealth by the controller/shareholder, and there will be an argument that any growth in the value of the company cannot be beneficially owned by the controller/shareholder.
- Where the controller/shareholder is introducing the assets to the company, it would be very helpful to have clear corporate documentation regarding where the beneficial interests in those assets lie.

19.6 The matrimonial home will probably be treated differently to any other property held by the company, and it will be difficult to avoid an inference that the home is held on trust for the occupier if they are also the controller of the company.

19.7 It must also be remembered that although the company's assets will be protected, the shareholding would be vulnerable. The following issues would assist:

- The company's governance documentation (preferably the articles of association, but if not then the shareholders' agreement) can be drafted so as to restrict transfers of shareholdings and to include compulsory transfer provisions which set the value of the shares reflecting a discount for a minority interest).
- The company could be based in a jurisdiction where enforcement of a share transfer order would be difficult.

19.8 It is worth noting that a client should co-operate with the financial remedy disclosure process. A lack of co-operation will give the impression to the court that there is a vulnerability to a case that the client is trying to hide, and the Supreme Court specifically endorsed the practice taken by the Family Division of making evidential assumptions against the person who is not co-operative.

19.9 If a trust owns shares in a FIC, the trust can provide another layer of protection in the event of a divorce. Although where a trust is used for protection, care needs to be taken to ensure that it is and remains a non-nuptial settlement as the courts do have power to vary a nuptial settlement.

19.10 A number of factors should be considered, including who are the beneficiaries, what is the purpose of the trust, who are the trustees and are they independent from the beneficiary. If a beneficiary is seen as being able to call upon trust assets as he or she wishes, the courts are more likely to regard the trust as a nuptial settlement.

19.11 Where asset protection is important the family should insist on members having pre or post marital agreements. This is the best way to provide asset protection and could be a requirement set out in the shareholders' agreement. Such agreements will be upheld by the court provided they are considered fair.

Chapter 20

Unlimited Companies and Privacy

20.1 Privacy is often a material concern for families, particularly where children and young adults are concerned. Wealth can attract undesirable attention, so being able to limit the amount of information that is publicly available is important.

20.2 Companies incorporated in England and Wales are registered at Companies House and certain information is freely available. The level of information available depends on the type of company, an unlimited company has lighter reporting obligations, making it an attractive form of company to use as a FIC.

20.3 An unlimited company has shares in just the same way as a limited company and will remain liable for its debts as long as the company has sufficient assets to meet its liabilities. If an unlimited company is unable to meet its liabilities, shareholders become liable for the debts of the company. In light of the risk of liability, the directors of a FIC should be careful about managing risk to ensure, as far as possible an unlimited company is never exposed to risks above its assets, or it maintains adequate insurance.

20.4 If the FIC intends to trade or acquire any assets, such as a property, which carry risks that could exceed its assets (subject to insurance), then it is sensible to consider using a limited company.

20.5 The key advantage of an unlimited company is the exemption from filing accounts at Companies House. This helps to keep the family's finances a little more private. This exemption will apply provided the unlimited company does not have a subsidiary or parent company that is a limited company.

20.6 Whilst the accounts remain private, the articles of association, details of shareholders, directors and people with significant control are all publically available whether or not a company is limited or unlimited.

20.7 An annual confirmation statement for any company (limited or unlimited) needs to be filed at Companies House. This replaced what used to be known as the annual return but serves the same purpose. One element of the confirmation statement is to list the shareholders of the company. Where shares are held in trust (including a bare trust) it is the name of the trustees that are recorded.

20.8 All companies must now maintain a register of 'People with significant control' ('PSC'). If a shareholder holds more than 25% of the shares, they are classified as a *person with significant control* and this information must be registered at Companies House in the PSC Register and on the confirmation statement. Where shares are held in a bare trust on behalf of minors, the trustees will be the relevant persons for the PSC but once the child turns 18, they will be the relevant person. It is worth remembering that you only have 14 days to update the register when there is a change of PSC. Given this register is publicly available on Companies House, it is always important to consider who should have 25% or less of the shares, to avoid having to go on to the PSC Register.

20.9 The nominal value of each share issued is visible on the Companies House website. Accordingly, if a shareholder subscribes £1 million in £1 shares, it will be seen that he/she has invested £1 million in the FIC. However, there is no requirement for an unlimited company to record any share premium on the shares and given no accounts are filed showing this information, it can be kept private. Therefore, if a shareholder invests £1 million in one million penny shares, all that is visible to an outsider is that the shareholder has invested at least £10,000. For this reason, some FICs may prefer to issue shares at a premium so as not to highlight the amount of share capital that has been invested. If a share premium is to be used, it is worth noting that subscriber shares cannot be issued at a premium.

20.10 Whilst having Redeemable Preference Shares can provide flexibility for a FIC, their existence is unhelpful from the perspective of privacy. Redeemable Preference Shares are normally redeemed at their nominal value, so the nominal value will reflect the amount subscribed

20.11 Provided the company was originally set up as unlimited, it can convert to limited status and vice versa but a company can only convert one way once. If an unlimited company is preferred it is advisable to form the company as unlimited so that the option to convert to limited liability status, should the nature of the business change, remains open.

20.12 An unlimited company also benefits from less onerous obligations under the *Companies Act 2006* should it wish to return capital to shareholders.

Chapter 21

Winding Up a FIC

21.1 If a FIC has come to the end of its useful life, the way to bring it to an end is to wind it up. When a company is wound up, it is deemed to dispose of all of its assets which will trigger a corporation tax charge on its total gains. Any unused capital losses will be lost on the winding up.

21.2 Surplus assets are then distributed to the shareholders in proportion to their capital rights. Distributions made in the course of a winding up are generally treated as a capital receipt in the hands of a shareholder.

21.3 With effect from 6 April 2016, the transaction in securities legislation (which applies to close companies) was extended to include a repayment of share capital or premium and a distribution in the course of a winding up. The rules were also extended to include some targeted anti-avoidance provisions for arrangements where a company is wound up but the individual carries on a trade or activity which is the same as, or similar to, that carried on by the company in a two year period (whether as an individual, in partnership or through another company in which he or she holds more than a 5% interest).

21.4 These rules should be borne in mind if a FIC is to be wound up with significant surplus profits or on a return of share capital. For example, if a FIC was established and the capital invested in a portfolio of investments, generating dividend income, which is not subject to corporation tax and gains which are. No distributions are made to shareholders. After a short period, say four years, the FIC is wound up and the entire profits are distributed to shareholders as part of the winding up. The shareholders have received an income tax advantage as all the accumulated profits are now taxed as a capital receipt at 20% instead of at dividend income tax rates of up to 38.1%. A challenge by HMRC under the transaction in securities rules has to be a possibility in such a situation. If there are concerns about the application of the transaction in securities legislation an advance clearance can be obtained from HMRC although no such clearance can be obtained for the targeted anti-avoidance provisions.

Chapter 22

Example Structures

EXAMPLE 1 – SIMPLE STRUCTURE

22.1 In this simple structure the four family members are all shareholders and hold 25% of the ordinary shares that have been issued. The ordinary shares all have a nominal value of £1 and carry an equal right to vote, income and capital.

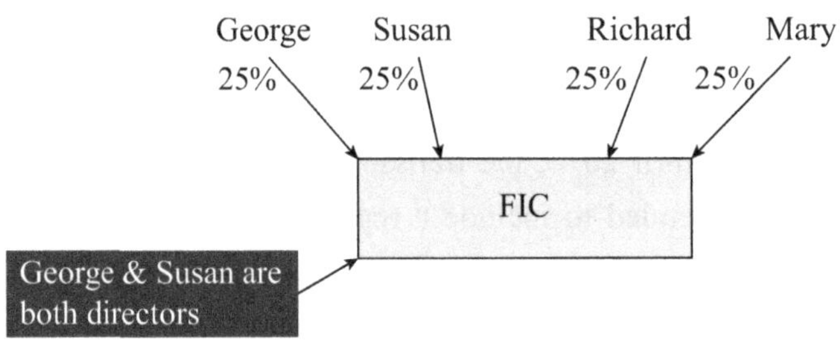

22.2 The share capital in the above company is:

Shareholder	Ordinary £1.00 shares	Percentage
George	500,000	25%
Susan	500,000	25%
Richard	500,000	25%
Mary	500,000	25%
	2,000,000	100%

22.3 In this example, George and Susan are the parents and they have formed the FIC, giving 25% of the shares to each of their children, Richard and Mary, who are both adults. The benefits of the structure are:

- George and Susan have made gifts totally £1 million reducing their estate for inheritance tax purposes, which after seven years, will fall out of account completely saving £400,000 in inheritance tax.

- George and Susan have retained a 50% interest but this does not give them control. On their death a valuation of the 50% interest will be needed (as they are a married couple) and half of that value will be included as an asset in each of their estates.[1] It is likely that they will get a discount on a 50% interest as it represents a minority interest saving further inheritance tax.
- Richard and Mary own exactly 25% of the shares and they will both get a more significant discount on their shares in the event of their death.
- Richard and Mary will not need to be named on the persons of significant control register at Companies House as they do not own more than a 25% interest.
- George and Susan are the directors and will make all the day to day decisions, including how to invest the funds and when and how much of any profits are to be distributed to the shareholders.
- Profits will accumulate in the FIC at corporate tax rates, which are more favourable to personal tax rates.
- Dividends are only paid when income is needed and the amount can be determined to maximise the use of personal allowances and lower tax bands (subject to the principle that each shareholder should only receive 25% of the profits at any time).
- George and Susan will involve Richard and Mary in the running of the FIC to help with their financial education. They may choose to do this formally through a committee, shareholders' meetings or more informally.
- Overall this is a simple, yet effective way of undertaking some estate planning and has the advantage of being simple to understand.

22.4 The disadvantages of this structure are:

- If all the income is needed to fund living expenses, overall the tax payable by the family may be increased due to the double layer of tax.
- The capital of £2 million invested in the FIC cannot be easily repaid to the family if needed.
- If George and Susan wish to make a material change to the FIC that requires a change of articles, Richard or Mary will have to give their consent.
- The value of the shares owned by Richard and Mary may be taken into account as a resource if they were to divorce.

[1] *IHTA 1984, s 161.*

EXAMPLE 2: INCLUDING A TRUST IN THE STRUCTURE

22.5 A family trust may be included in the structure:

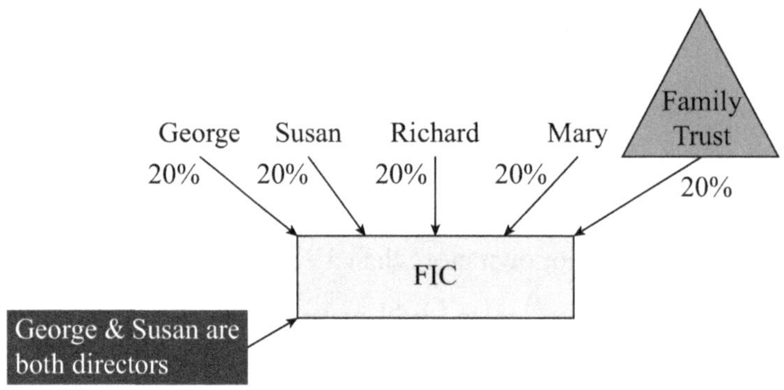

22.6 The share structure may now look like this:

Shareholder	Ordinary £1.00 shares	Percentage
George	175,000	8.75%
Susan	175,000	8.75%
Richard	500,000	25.00%
Mary	500,000	25.00%
Family Trust	650,000	32.50%
	2,000,000	100.00%

22.7 By including a trust as an additional shareholder, George and Susan have been able to increase the level of estate planning. They fund the family trust with cash up to their full unused nil rate bands of £325,000 each. After seven years the inheritance tax saving will now have increased to £660,000.

22.8 There are a number of advantages of using the family trust in the structure, they are:

- the shares held in the family trust may be used for future grandchildren;
- the level of gifts has increased without increasing the number of shares held by Richard and Mary;
- the shares in the family trust can be better protected from the impact of a family divorce;
- George and Susan will retain control over the voting rights attached to the shares in the trust, although they will of course have to ensure they only exercise those votes to approve matters that will benefit their beneficiaries, and
- if Richard or Mary need income above their entitlement to 25% of the profits, dividends can be paid to the trust and the income used for their benefit (assuming they are beneficiaries of the trust).

EXAMPLE 3: MORE COMPLEX STRUCTURE WITH ALPHABET AND REDEEMABLE PREFERENCE SHARES

22.9 If George and Susan wanted to have more flexibility, they may choose:

- for each shareholder to have a separate class of ordinary shares to provide some flexibility on the timing and quantum of dividends payable to each shareholder, and
- to issue some redeemable preference shares providing an ability to return capital to shareholders more easily.

22.10 The share capital could be:

Shareholder	Ordinary £1.00 shares	Share class	Redeemable preference shares	Percentage
George	43,750	A	131,250	8.75%
Susan	43,750	B	131,250	8.75%
Richard	125,000	C	375,000	25.00%
Mary	125,000	D	375,000	25.00%
Family Trust	162,500	E	487,500	32.50%
	500,000		1,500,000	100.00%

22.11 The redeemable preference shares would have a nominal value of £1 each and would be redeemable at the discretion of the directors. The shares may have a right to interest but do not need to in this example as each shareholder has an equal proportion of ordinary shares to redeemable preference shares. All the rights would be set in the FIC's articles.

22.12 The advantage of such shares is that the directors can return capital to shareholders more easily by electing to redeem the shares. On redemption the shares would be cancelled. The shareholder would receive their original subscription price of £1 together with interest (if any). To the extent the shareholder receives back their original £1 investment, no tax charge will arise subject to the application of the transaction in securities rules outlined above.

22.13 One example where redeemable preference shares may be helpful, is if the founders of the FIC failed to survive seven years following the original gift of funds to establish the FIC. If the deaths happened quickly, then the FIC is unlikely to have generated much in the way of profit to be able to pay a dividend to help fund the tax. Where the FIC has no profits, redeeming preference shares may be a useful way to return capital funds to shareholders. It is worth noting that the process for redeeming shares is easier in an unlimited company compared to a limited company.

EXAMPLE 4: STRUCTURE WITH VOTING AND NON-VOTING SHARES

22.14 If George and Susan wanted absolute control they may decide they want to alter voting rights as follows.

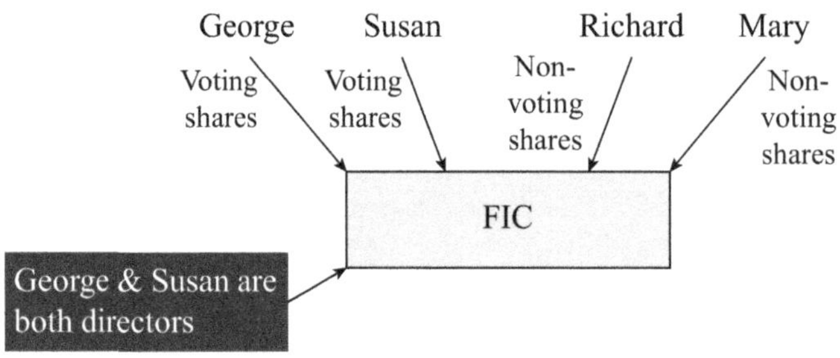

22.15 In the above example, George and Susan have retained all the voting rights between them, giving them absolute control of the FIC. This structure may have some attraction but it must be remembered that the voting rights will have a material value, reducing the estate planning achieved by the structure. It also means, George and Susan will have to consider carefully who inherits the shares given the control they have.

22.16 If George and Susan decide to put the voting shares in trust, care will be needed to ensure the value of the shares is within their available nil rate band allowances. Furthermore, if the shares have no right to income and their value increases such that ten-year charges will arise in the trust, consideration will have to be given on how those tax charges will be paid.

EXAMPLE 5: FUNDING WITH DEBT

22.17 In this example, George and Susan choose to fund the FIC with debt rather than share capital:

Shareholder	**Ordinary £1.00 shares**	**Share class**	**Percentage**	**Debt**
George	1,000	A	10.0%	335,000
Susan	1,000	B	10.0%	335,000
Richard	1,500	C	15.0%	335,000
Mary	1,500	D	15.0%	335,000
Family Trust	5,000	E	50.0%	650,000
	10,000		100.0%	1,990,000

22.18 The terms of the debt will need careful drafting to ensure that George and Susan, as directors, can control repayment. It would be recommended that the debt carries an entitlement to a commercial rate of interest to ensure the arrangement is regarded as commercial. The interest can be accumulated and paid only when debt is repaid or earlier at the discretion of the directors.

22.19 The use of debt creates an opportunity for the easier return of capital to the shareholders. It may also be tax efficient if the FIC is able to claim a corporation tax deduction for the payment of interest. In this example the family trust is able to have a larger proportion of the share capital but due to funding restraints take a smaller proportion of the debt.

Structure Using Growth Shares

22.20 When considering the capital rights attaching to the ordinary shares, George and Susan may consider it appropriate to allow Richard and Mary's shares to have a greater share in the growth of the FIC than their own shares. This will reduce or even cap the value of George and Susan's shares. The shares rights may be:

> 'On a return of capital on a winding up, reduction of capital or otherwise the assets of the company remaining after the payment of its liabilities shall be applied as follows:
>
> - first, in paying to the holders of the Ordinary Shares (as if the same constituted one class of Share) the subscription price for each relevant Ordinary Share (which has been duly paid);
> - secondly, the remaining assets available for distribution up to the first £2.5 million shall be distributed amongst the holders of all Ordinary Shares (as if the same constituted one class of Share) in proportion to the number of Ordinary Shares held by such holders; and
> - finally the remaining assets available for distribution above £2.5 million shall be distributed to the holders of the Ordinary C Shares and Ordinary D Shares to be divided pro rata in proportion to the number of Ordinary C Shares and Ordinary D Shares held by such holders.'

22.21 By using growth shares, George and Susan will have capped the value of their shares, which will assist further with their estate planning. The disadvantage, is that the share capital is more complex, which may make further planning more difficult. It may have been simpler for George and Susan to just retain less shares.